THE Alberta Trivia Book

THE Alberta TriviaBook

DON BLAKE

LONE PINE

The Publisher:
Lone Pine Publishing
#206 10426-81 Avenue
Edmonton, Alberta, Canada
T6E 1X5

Canadian Cataloguing in Publication Data

Blake, Don, 1935 -
The Alberta trivia book

ISBN 0-919433-71-5

1. Alberta - Miscellanea. I. Title.
FC3661.B62 1990   971.23 C90-091076-3
F1076.B62 1990

Cover Design: Yuet Chan
Editorial and Production: Jane Spalding
Printing: Reliable Printing Ltd., Edmonton, Alberta, Canada

The publisher gratefully acknowledges the assistance of the Federal
Department of Communications, Alberta Culture and Multiculturalism,
the Canada Council and the Alberta Foundation for the Literary Arts in
the publication of this book.

To D.D.

CONTENTS

ACKNOWLEDGEMENTS

To my willing and able assistant and partner, Donna Nemedy, to Phil Makow for his artwork, to Pix-A-Color of Edmonton for photo processing and to a great number of people all over the province who gave me information, directions and advice, thank you all very much.
I would also like to thank information officer Major Tremblay at CFB Edmonton and Carol and Daryl at the Alberta Provincial Map Office.

Personnel at these places also helped in the compilation of material for this book:

Alberta Forest Service
Alberta Government Telephones (Vista 33)
Alberta Sports Council
Alberta Wheat Pool
Bad Heart Cultural Association
Canada Post Corporation
Canada's Aviation Hall of Fame
Canadian Parks Service, Jasper National Park (for their photo of Mt. Columbia)
College of Physicians
Department of Education

Department of Municipal Affairs
Edmonton Convention Centre
Edmonton Power Corporation Ltd.
Edmonton Public Library
Edmonton Space Sciences Centre
Town of Edson
Town of Grand Centre
Historic Sites and Monuments Board of Canada
Historic Sites Services, Alberta Culture (for their photo of Fort McMurray Oil Sands Interpretive Centre)
Legislative Library
National Parks
Obed Mountain Coal Company
County of Parkland

Petro-Canada
Provincial Archives of Alberta
Provincial Government Protocol Office
Provincial Historic Sites
Royal Canadian Mounted Police
TransAlta Utilities
Transportation Canada
Travel Alberta Tourist Information Offices
Tyrrell Museum of Anthropology
Wajax Industries Mining Division
Weather Office (Edmonton)
West Edmonton Mall (WEM) Public Relations Department
Western Canada Lottery Corporation

Author's note:

You may have noticed on a previous page my publisher's acknowledgements. I hope this did not leave the impression that I was in any way a beneficiary of any such assistance. Apparently Alberta Culture does not view this book as a cultural or historical work or of any benefit to Alberta's "Take an Alberta Break" tourist promotion programs. On behalf of myself and many other writers contributing to Alberta's cultural awareness, and promoting Alberta as a destination of quality, I wish to express some doubts as to procedures used in their funding policies.

- Don Blake

FOREWORD

While Alberta is considered the westernmost of the three prairie provinces, it is actually much more than that. The original French explorers applied the name prairie, meaning grasslands, to the great plains area. Webster's Dictionary defines prairie as "an extensive treeless tract of level or slightly undulating land covered with tall coarse grass." Alberta has mountains, hills, forests, rivers and lakes as well as prairie.

Henderson's Alberta Directory of 1911 says: "The natural features of Alberta combine the beauties of prairie and mountain scenery. For three hundred miles open and wooded plains spread out in vast level reaches, and then climb over softly rounded mounds that grow higher and change till they break into jagged points and serried ridges and at last rest upon the base of the Rocky Mountains."

The following is from an article by H.H. Newcomb of the Calgary Automobile Club, which was printed in Wrigley's Alberta Directory in 1920:

"See Alberta First" should be the slogan of every man who is a motorist. When he has seen Alberta, and knows something of his own province he is then prepared to travel into other parts. We say so because it is an unfortunate fact that so many people travel into other provinces, who are unable to say very much about the province from which they hail. We all know from experience, that a traveller from any other place is always asked about his town, city or province. Be prepared with a first-hand knowledge of what your province contains, one never knows how your little boost will help out. It is often the means of bringing in business that would otherwise never come but for the information given at the time it is required. Alberta is worth talking about.

This same book also noted "The Kodak-er is never at a loss in Alberta." The Travel Alberta Accommodation Guide explains it this way: "Alberta contains the greatest variety of geographical features of any Canadian province," and is "a magnificent land with every natural feature except an ocean."

Here then are the five Ws of this magnificent land known as Alberta.

FLAGS AND EMBLEMS

Alberta was named after H.R.H. Princess Louise Caroline Alberta (1848-1939), fourth daughter of Queen Victoria and wife of the Marquis of Lorne (governor general of Canada from 1878 to 1883). In 1882 the area was designated a provisional district of the North-West Territories, and on September 1, 1905 became a province of the Dominion of Canada.

The motto of Alberta is "Fortis et Liber," which means strong and free.

The flag of Alberta

The flag of Alberta is actually the shield from the provincial coat of arms on a blue background. The flag is twice as long as it is wide, and the shield is positioned in the centre at seven elevenths of the flag's width. It was adopted on June 1st, 1968.

In 1984 the province adopted blue and gold (or deep yellow) as the official provincial colours.

The wild rose (*Rosa acicularis*) was adopted as the floral emblem of Alberta in 1930. It may be found growing in abundance in almost all parts of Alberta.

Princess Louise Caroline Alberta

The Alberta Coat of Arms

Wild rose

Lodgepole pine

Through a province-wide vote in 1977, the children of Alberta selected the great horned owl (*Budo virginianus*) as the official bird of the province. Legislation to this effect was passed on May 3, 1977. The great horned owl is found year-round throughout the province. This bird symbolizes our concern for the future of wildlife.

Through the efforts of the Junior Forest Warden Association of Alberta, the lodgepole pine (*Pinus contorta* variety *latifolia*) was declared the tree of Alberta on May 30, 1984.

Petrified wood was named the stone of Alberta in 1977, thanks to the efforts of the Alberta Federation of Rock Clubs.

Inspired by efforts of the Edmonton Rehabilitation Society for the Handicapped, Alberta Tartan was officially recognized by an act of legislation in 1961. The colours of the tartan are: green, representing Alberta's forests; gold, representing our wheat fields; blue, representing Alberta's skies and lakes; pink, for the wild rose; and black, representing Alberta's coal and petroleum industries.

HISTORY

About 570 million years ago most of Alberta was part of a large tropical inland ocean.

About 225 million years ago the first dinosaurs appeared.

About 70 million years ago the land began rising, a movement which resulted in the formation of the Rocky Mountains.

About 65 million years ago the first birds appeared.

About 250,000 years ago the ice was about 1.6 metres thick over central Alberta.

The last ice age, the retreat of which began about 13,000 years ago, created the soils and current river systems of the land as we know it today.

The oldest verified (or accepted) site of human habitation in Alberta is at Vermilion Lakes, and is about 11,000 years old. There is a possibility of a site about 25,000 years old in the Crowsnest Pass area.

The Sibbald area in southeastern Alberta also contains evidence of prehistoric habitation dating back 11,000 years.

Archaeological digs at Lake Minne-wanka have found evidence of human habitation dating back 10,000 years.

The tops of the Cypress Hills were left untouched by the last glacial period. There is evidence here of human habitation 7,000 years ago.

The Strathcona Archaeological Centre is the site of an excavation of a 5000-year-old prehistoric native site. During the summer months visitors can watch archaeologists at work here and can even volunteer as assistants. Phone 427-9487 (in Edmonton) for more information.

Display at Camp Yo Wo Ch As

One of the highest concentrations of prehistoric archaeological sites in Alberta is in the Waterton Lakes National Park.

The first professional archaeological dig in Alberta was at Head-Smashed-In Buffalo Jump in 1948. The site, near Lethbridge, was excavated by a team from the University of New Mexico.

Display at Camp Yo Wo Ch As

Anthony Henday was the first white man to visit what is now Alberta and to see the Rocky Mountains. The year was 1754 and he was travelling west, from Fort York on Hudson's Bay, a trip of 1920 kilometres by canoe. He entered Alberta on September 11, at a point about 14 kilometres northeast of the location of today's town of Chauvin. He recorded in his diary: "Level land, few woods, and plenty of good water . . . . Indians killed eight Waskasew [elk]." He was exploring for the Hudson's Bay Company and thus began Alberta's recorded history. It is thought he wintered with a band of Cree in the area of present-day Edmonton, and it was from the high ground of Antler Ridge, just north of Innisfail, where Anthony Henday became the first white man to see the Rocky Mountains.

Central southeast Alberta was first viewed and explored by Peter Fidler from 1792 to 1801. He also discovered the rich coal deposits along the Red Deer River in 1793.

Peter Pond of the North West Company established the first fur trading post in Alberta in 1778, on the Athabasca River. Fort Chipewyan was established nearby in 1788, on Lake Athabasca, and today it is the oldest continuously occupied settlement in Alberta.

It was from Fort Chipewyan that Alexander Mackenzie made two of his most famous journeys: down the great river that now bears his name in 1789; and up the Peace River and through the mountains to the Pacific Ocean in 1793. This trip made him the first white man to cross the North American continent by land.

Clerk's quarters building at Victoria Settlement.

Alberta's southern boundary (the 49th parallel) was established in 1818 from the east to the continental divide in the Rocky Mountains. (In 1846 this line was extended to the Pacific Ocean.) This line was laid out by the International Boundary Commission to separate the lands or territories of the United States and Great Britain. The boundary between Canada and the United States is 8,891 kilometres long and is maintained by a network, established by both countries, of 1,000 survey control stations along its length. Boundary markers are spaced at distances of 1.6 to 2.4 kilometres. The Canada - United States boundary is just off the 49th parallel by about 244 metres (800 ft.) at the Douglas, B.C./ Blaine, Washington crossing. This

error is in the favour of the United States. Near Coutts, AB and Sweetgrass, Montana, it is out about 366 metres (1,200 ft.) but in this case the error is in Canada's favour. Overall, the boundary is about 24 - 25 metres (80 ft.) in Canada's favour. These errors were the result of gravity anomalies that scientists were unaware of at the time. However, the legal boundary is the one in place.

The Palliser Expedition of 1857, headed by Captain John Palliser, was commissioned by the British government to "explore and report" on the potential of the prairie region. The main reason behind this expedition was to settle the question of whether the Hudson's Bay Company Charter should be renewed.

THE PEACE RIVER

From its headwaters in the mountains of British Columbia, the waters of the mighty Peace River flow through this valley on their way to the Arctic Ocean. The river is so named because it was along these banks that a peace between the warring Cree and Beaver Indians was concluded. Travelled first by Indians and fur traders, and later by missionaries, gold seekers and settlers, the river has served as a highway for the development of Northern Alberta.

The oldest building still on its original site in Alberta is the Hudson's Bay Company's clerks quarters at Fort Victoria (between Edmonton and Cold Lake). It was built in 1864.

On November 1 of 1869, the Canadian government purchased the entire HBC territory, from Manitoba to the Rocky Mountains, including all of the future province of Alberta.

The first, and most notorious, whiskey trading post in Alberta was established in 1869 for the purpose of trading guns and "firewater" to the Indians in exchange for buffalo robes and furs. Fort Whoop-Up was a pretty wild place and because of this the North-West Mounted Police force was formed, and in 1874 arrived to bring law and order to the Canadian West. The fort is located west of Lethbridge.

In 1870 all of the area between Manitoba and the Rocky Mountains was organized as the North-West Territories of Canada, with headquarters first at Winnipeg, then at Battleford and lastly at Regina.

The Peace Hills, near Wetaskiwin, were so named because the Cree and Blackfoot made peace here in 1867. In 1927 a monument was erected near Wetaskiwin to commemorate this event.

Peace Hills Cairn

After the signing of Treaty No. 7 at Blackfoot Crossing on September 22, 1877, the Plains people settled into three bands: the South Band, under Chief Crowfoot's leadership, settled along the river south of Cluny; the Central Band, under Iron Shield, settled south of Gleichen; and Chief Old Sun and the North Band settled in the river valley to the west. Treaty No. 7 ensured peace with the settlers and cleared the way for the railway to be brought through without any problems. The Blackfoot Cultural Centre at the crossing depicts the heritage of the local tribes.

In an 1885 Indian uprising, nine people were left dead at what is now the Frog Lake Massacre Historic Site, north of Lloydminster. The site is about 3 kilometres east of the Frog Lake Store.

The great influx of settlers to the western prairies, which began in the late 1800s, resulted in the formation of Alberta as a province.

By act of parliament Alberta became a province of the Dominion of Canada on September 1, 1905. The next day A.C. Rutherford was installed as the first premier.

The federal government transferred jurisdiction of lands and natural resources to the province in 1930.

Northern Alberta is full of forests, lakes and rivers. Once a resource for fur traders, it is now valued for its deposits of heavy oils, the largest in the world.

Jubilee Memorial

The Jubilee Memorial, originally located in front of the main entrance to the Legislature Building, was unveiled and dedicated by the Right Honourable Louis St. Laurent, prime minister of Canada, on September 7, 1955, in commemoration of the inauguration of the Province of Alberta on September 1, 1905. This was Alberta's golden jubilee. In 1988 this memorial was moved approximately 90 metres to the east to make way for the reflection pool which was built in front of the Legislature Building.

The name Blackfoot, or Sisksikawa in the language of this Plains Indian tribe, refers to the black moccasin soles of these people, which were painted or darkened by the ashes of prairie fires.

In 1911 the Blood Indian Reserve, southeast of Macleod, was the largest reserve in Canada at approximately 1425 square kilometres.

The Blood Indian Reserve west of Cardston, Alberta, is the largest Indian reserve in Canada today. It is in the Rocky Mountain foothills.

Kinosoo totem poles

This Kwakuitl totem pole was presented to the people of Alberta by the province of British Columbia in B.C.'s centennial year.

The Pakashan Indian Reserve, in the Lesser Slave Lake area, is the smallest reserve in Canada. This reserve is run as a farming operation by the Chalifoux family, and they have operated it as such since its formation back in the 1800s.

The Kinosoo Totem Poles can be found at the end of Highway 28 overlooking the shores of Cold Lake, Alberta's seventh largest lake. The two cedar poles, which are 6.6 metres high, were carved by Chief Ovide Jacko of the Cold Lake Indian Reserve. The signs and symbols on the poles were designed to resemble those used by the ancestors of the Cold Lake Indians.

The old Indian custom of using tree graves is no longer permitted in Alberta, but some old tree graves can still be found. A sixty-five year old grave, probably one of the last, is located on the Old Mackenzie Highway about 200 metres from Indian Cabin Store. This ancient custom involved placing the dead in a hollowed-out log and hoisting the log into a tree.

PEOPLE

The population of Alberta in April of 1987 was estimated to be 2,378,100. This was equal to 9.2% of the population of Canada and it gave a density of 3.7 persons per square kilometre. *The Commerce News* [Edmonton Chamber of Commerce] reports that "If Alberta [were] as densely populated as Japan, we'd have 200 million people living here instead of 2.3 million."

The population of Alberta consists of the following ethnic backgrounds: British - 44%, German - 14%, Slavic - 11%, Scandinavian - 7%, French - 6%, Other - 18%. There are over 40 different cultural and ethnic groups in Alberta, and of the total population, 117,000 may be categorized as being part of a visible minority. Over 60,000 are Native Canadians.

Alberta's population is 77.3% urban, 14% rural nonfarming and 8.7% farming.

In 1986 Alberta had 44,010 births, 13,690 deaths and 20,430 marriages.

The most common language spoken in Alberta is English, used by approximately 91.7% of the population, followed by French at 1.3%, and all others combined at 7%.

Alberta has the highest divorce rate per capita in Canada. In 1986, Statistics Canada figures show 9,396 divorces per 100,000 married couples. This was up about 16% over the 1985 figure of 8,102 divorces per 100,000 couples.

(Newfoundland had the lowest rate in Canada, at 469 divorces per 100,000 couples.)

In 1977 Calgary was the divorce capital of Canada with more divorces per capita than any city in the country.

According to Statistics Canada, Alberta leads the rest of the provinces in volunteer participation, with 706,000 registered volunteers throughout the province. Within Alberta, Edmonton has the highest volunteer participation rate at 38.2% of the population. (Saskatoon has the highest rate of all major cities in Canada at 44.5% — Edmonton is second.)

Most major cities and towns have some form of Light-Up contest during the Christmas season. In Edmonton the 1988 winners were Terry and Nellie Sargent. The Sargent house and property were lit up with 4,500 lights which Mr. Sargent bought with money saved by quitting smoking. The first prize was $500.

Cynthia Kereluk of Edmonton was the winner of the 1984 Miss Canada Pageant. She now has her own show on CFRN-TV, "Everyday Workout," which is seen by about 42 million North American households.

Eldon Mandelin, of Rocky Mountain House, has the largest collection of barbed wire in Canada. It includes some of the first barbed wire, which was made in 1867.

ROYAL VISITS

Unfortunately space does not permit a complete listing of all the royal visitors to Alberta — there have been many. The following is a brief list of the more notable visits:

The first appearance by royalty in Alberta was in 1901 when the Duke and Duchess of Cornwall and York visited the area.

The first reigning monarch to visit Canada, and Alberta, was King George VI, who came in 1939. The highlight of this royal visit to Edmonton on June 2, 1939, was the motorcade down Kingsway, formerly Portage Avenue, (renamed for this occasion). At this time Kingsway was referred to as the widest, longest paved street in North America without any buildings along it. To accommodate the thousands of spectators, two miles of bleachers were constructed, and the *Edmonton Bulletin* reported "The bleachers standing there are said to be the longest grandstand in the world and will be an outstanding feature of Edmonton's welcome to the royal couple."

VISITS OF ROYALTY TO ALBERTA

1959	Queen Elizabeth II
1973	Queen Elizabeth II
1978	Queen Elizabeth II
1985	Crown Prince Vajiralongkorn of Thailand
1985	Queen Elizabeth, The Queen Mother
1987	Pope John Paul II
1987	The Prince and Princess of Japan
1987	King Olav V of Norway
1988	Queen Beatrice of the Netherlands
1988	King Juan Carlos, of Spain
1988	King Carl Gustav, of Sweden
1988	Prince Rainier of Monaco
1989	King Hussein of Jordan

PLACES

Alberta has some very interesting and intriguing place names. Some names, I hope, do not reflect the outlook of the people of the area, such as Dismal Creek, Gloomy Creek, or Quarrel, while other names, I hope, do, such as Happy Hollow, Paradise Valley and Makepeace. Some names can put your imagination to work, like Mystery Lake, Spirit Island or Pile of Bones Creek. Many geographical features are simply descriptive, such as Stairway Peak or Table Mountain. Listening Mountain was so named because it resembles an ear. Pyramid Lake was named not because it looked like a pyramid, but rather after Pyramid Mountain which does. There are animal and bird names (Turtle Mountain and Raven River), plant names, foreign names and names from mythology. And there are a great many native names, such as Kakwa (Porcupine) Mountain, and Opi-mi-now-wa-sioo, which translates to Cooking Lake.

In Alberta, besides foothills there are also Kneehills, Handhills, Nose Hills and Hairy Hill.

Alberta, according to Municipal Affairs, " . . . is the only province in Canada to provide for separate Métis settlements, and there are eight of these within the province."

The rivalry between Edmonton and Calgary began in 1905 with the question of which city should be capital of the new province of Alberta.

CITIES AND TOWNS

On December 20, 1911, Alberta became the third province of Canada to establish a Department of Municipal Affairs.

There are four types of rural municipal areas in Alberta: counties, municipal districts, improvement districts and special areas. In 1987, the rural areas of Alberta consisted of 30 counties, 20 municipal districts, 19 improvement districts, and 3 special areas. Incorporated urban centres (cities, towns, villages, and summer villages) are separate municipal units and are not part of a rural municipal area.

Incorporated status means that a municipal corporation is formed under provincial legislation, is governed by a locally elected council and is responsible for providing local services within the municipal boundaries. Within Alberta, cities, towns, villages, summer villages, municipal districts, and counties are all incorporated. Improvement districts and special areas are unincorporated and are administered by the provincial government. Alberta now has 16 cities, 108 towns, 122 villages, and 50 summer villages.

SLOGANS AND MOTTOS OF ALBERTA COMMUNITIES

Northwestern Alberta

Beaverlodge is the "Gateway to the Monkman Pass."
Fairview is the "Heart of the Peace."
Falher is the "Honey Capital of Canada."
Grande Prairie is the "Home of the Trumpeter Swan."
High Level is the "Gateway to the Northwest Territories."
Hythe is "The Town of Flowing Wells."
Manning is the "Land of the Mighty Moose."

McLennan is the "Land of Golden Opportunity," and the self-proclaimed "Bird Capital of Canada."

St. Paul is "Home of the Flying Saucer Landing Pad."

Wanham is "Home of the Grizzly Bear Prairie Museum" and also "Home of the Provincial Plowing Championships."

Whitecourt is "Where Even the Rivers Meet" and the "Snowmobile Capital of Alberta."

Northeastern Alberta

Fort McMurray became a city in 1980 and, as that was the year of Alberta's 75th anniversary, it became known as the Jubilee City.

Grimshaw is "mile zero of the Mackenzie Highway."

Rycroft is the "Hub of the Peace."

Sexsmith is called "The Grain Capital of Alberta."

Central

Camrose is Alberta's "Rose City."

Donalda is "Canada's Lamp Capital," because it has a large lamp museum.

Edmonton is: "The Gateway to the North," "The Oil Capital of Canada," "Canada's Festival City," "The Shopping Centre Capital of Canada," "The Indoor Rodeo Capital of Canada" and "The City of Champions."

Edson is "the town with a future."

Hinton is "Gateway to the Rockies."

Onoway is the "Hub of the Highways."

Spruce Grove is "planned for tomorrow."

Vegreville is "The Home of the Giant Pysanka" (Ukranian Easter Egg).

Wildwood is "Home of the Snow Goose," and also "The Bingo Capital of Canada." (There are more than 140 regularly scheduled bingos here — more than in any other village its size in Canada.)

CITIES OF ALBERTA

Airdrie
Elevation - 1,082 m
Area - 22 sq. km
Population - 10,461

Drumheller
Elevation - 686 m
Area - 25 sq. km
Population - 6,366

Fort Saskatchewan
Elevation - 625 m
Area - 34 sq. km
Population - 11,983

Lethbridge
Elevation - 914 m
Area - 124 sq. km
Population - 60,610

Red Deer
Elevation - 860 m
Area - 53 sq. km
Population - 54,309

Spruce Grove
Elevation - 705 m
Area - 20 sq. km
Population - 11,918

Calgary
Elevation - 1,049 m
Area - 539 sq. km
Population - 647,285

Edmonton
Elevation - 668 m
Area - 699 sq. km
Population - 576,249

Grande Prairie
Elevation - 655 m
Area - 42 sq. km
Population - 26,471

Lloydminster
Elevation - 649 m
Area - 39 sq. km
Population - 10,201

St. Albert
Elevation - 672 m
Area - 35 sq. km
Population - 37,008

Wetaskiwin
Elevation - 762 m
Area - 14 sq. km
Population - 10,103

Camrose
Elevation - 741 km
Area - 25 sq. km
Population - 12,968

Fort McMurray
Elevation - 300 m
Area - 64 sq. km
Population - 34,949

Leduc
Elevation - 728 m
Area - 23 sq. km
Population - 13,126

Medicine Hat
Elevation - 668 m
Area - 104 sq. km
Population - 41,804

Southwestern Alberta

Acme is "the rural recreational capital of Alberta."

Airdrie is "Alberta's friendliest city."

Calgary, around the turn of the century, was known as "Sandstone City." Today it is more commonly referred to as "Cowtown."

Cardston calls itself the "Temple City."

Jasper is "The Gem of the Rockies."

Lake Louise is also called the "Gem of the Canadian Rockies."

Olds was once known as "Hay City."

Pincher Creek is the "Gateway to the Rockies."

Southeastern Alberta

Bassano calls itself the "best little town in the West by a dam site."

Caster is "Home of Paddy the Beaver."

Chauvin is "home of the world's largest softball."

Delia is the "Gateway to the Scenic Handhills."

Drumheller is the "dinosaur capital of the world."

Elnora is "where friendship is a way of life."

Hanna is the "Home of the Wild Goose."

Hardisty is "The Flag Capital of the World."

Lethbridge is the "Irrigation Capital of Canada."

Linden is "The Rural Industrial Capital of Alberta."

Lloydminster is known as "Canada's Border City."

Magrath is "The Garden City."

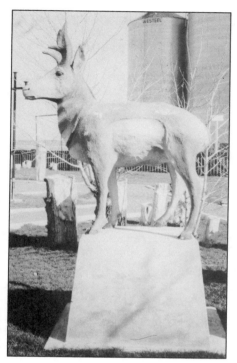

Medicine Hat is known as "Gas City."
Oyen is "Home of the Pronghorn
Antelope."
Three Hills, depending on where or
what you are reading, is the: "Wheat
Capital of Alberta," "Wheat Capital of
Canada" or "Wheat Capital of the
World."
Trochu is the "Hub of a Progressive
Community."
Vulcan is "The Wheat Capital of
Canada."

MORE ABOUT ALBERTA PLACES

Northwestern

The oldest Danish settlement in
western Canada is Dickson. This
hamlet is also home to Canada's first
Danish Lutheran congregation.

A man named Shaw was a Hudson's
Bay Company factor in charge of the
district around Lesser Slave Lake. The
book *2,000 Place Names of Alberta*
quotes Charles Mair, saying Mr. Shaw
appeared " . . . to be a man of many

eccentricities, one of which was the
cultivation, à la Chinois, of a very long
fingernail, which he used as a spoon to
eat his egg." Shaw Point on the north
shore of Lesser Slave Lake is named
for this man.

May Lake, McConachie Lake, and
McMullen Lake are all named after
pioneers of flying in Canada's north-
land.

Fort Vermilion is one of the oldest
European settlements in Alberta. The
North West Company built a post near
here in 1788 but it was not until 1831
that the fort was established. The town
celebrated its 200th birthday during the
first week of August in 1988.

Northeastern

The village of Bon Accord, Alberta,
was named after the motto of the city
of Aberdeen in Scotland, which is
"Bon Accord" or, in English, "good
wishes."

Cold Lake is one of the clearest and
deepest lakes in Alberta and it also
contains the greatest variety of fish
species of any lake in Alberta.

Fort Chipewyan is Alberta's oldest
settlement, dating from the late
eighteenth century. It is an isolated
settlement which can be reached only
by plane or boat, and is located on
Lake Athabasca. There are archaeological sites in the area. During its
early days, Fort Chip was called the fur
trade capital of the Northwest.

Fort McMurray is surrounded by
water, as it sits just inside the intersec-
tions of the Clearwater, Hangingstone,
Horse and Athabasca rivers. Fort
McMurray originated with the fur
trade, later had a salt plant, was
occupied by U.S. troops during World
War II, and is now the site of the
development of the Athabasca tar
sands. The Pond Hotel is named after
one of Alberta's earliest explorers (see
People chapter).

Fort McMurray has one of the youngest
average populations in Canada. It is
also the northernmost city in Alberta.

Hairy Hill is a place where buffalo
once shed their hair. It is located east
of Edmonton.

Meanook is claimed to be the geographic centre of Alberta. Meanook is
an Indian word meaning good camping
place.

Central

Devon was named after the geological
formation it sits upon: the Devonian
Formation. It was within this feature
that the Leduc oil field was discovered.

Drayton Valley was the first govern-
ment-planned model town in Alberta.

Edmonton is named after Edmonton,
England. This came about when the
Hudson's Bay Company built a trading
post to compete with the nearby Fort
Augustus (near today's Fort Saskatchewan) of the North West Company. The deputy governor of the
HBC, Sir James Winter-Lake, named
this post Edmonton House after his
hometown in 1795. It soon became a
main point in the HBC network.
Edmonton became a town in 1892, and
a city in 1904. Today the city covers an
area of 70,152 hectares.

Edmonton has more sunshine and
more parkland than any other major
city in Canada.

The Chinatown Gate at 102 Avenue
and 97 Street in Edmonton was
dedicated in a ceremony on October
24, 1987, as a symbol of friendship
between Edmonton and her sister city,
Harbin, in China. The gate is 12 metres
high and 23 metres wide, crossing
Harbin Road, which is a section of 102
Avenue renamed. You can roll the ball
in the lion's mouth for good luck.

The giant pysanka at Vegreville

Kapasiwin, established in 1918, is the oldest summer village in Alberta.

Stony Plain was incorporated in 1908. The year before, Sheriff Umbach chained a railroad locomotive to the tracks in this town to force the railroad company to pay its taxes.
Stony Plain's sister town is Shikaoi, Japan.

Strathcona County is named after Lord Strathcona. The history of the county as an organized political area began in 1893, with the Clover Bar area being declared by the territorial government in Regina as Statute Labour District

The lion at Edmonton's Chinatown Gate

Number Two. It was in fact the first self-governing area in Alberta. Strathcona amalgamated with the city of Edmonton in 1912.

Vegreville's claim to fame lies with its giant pysanka (Ukranian easter egg). It was constructed in 1974 commemorating the 100th anniversary of the arrival of the RCMP in Alberta. It is over 7 metres long and 5.5 metres wide, weighs 2,270 kilograms, and is made from 3,500 pieces of aluminum. The design tells the story of the area's settlers, their strong faith, the good harvest and the protection received from the RCMP. Vegreville's annual Ukranian festival is held in July.

Calgary skyline

Wildwood is the smallest community in Canada to have its own trade coin recognized by numismatists.

Southwestern

Airdrie's motto may be "the friendliest city in Alberta," but a few hundred years ago, when the Shoshoni Indians were attempting to move in on this territory of the Blackfoot, there were many battles here.

In Henderson's Alberta Directory for 1911, Banff is described as " . . . a medicinal watering place and pleasure resort."

The longest gondola ride in Canada is from Banff up to Sunshine Village, which is nestled high in the mountains above.

The locality of Bennett was named after R.B. Bennett. From his law practice in Calgary he became a MLA in 1909 and held this position until 1911. He then entered federal politics and became an MP. He was prime minister of Canada from 1930 to 1935.

Calgary - The name of this city comes from the Gaelic word "Calgarry" meaning clear, running water. It was also the name of Colonel J.F. Macleod's family estate on the Isle of Mull. He was the assistant commissioner of the North-West Mounted Police when they established Fort Calgary at the junction of the Bow and Elbow rivers in 1875.

Calgary's Chinatown is the largest chinese district on the prairies and second largest in western Canada. (Vancouver's Chinatown is the largest in Canada, and is also second largest in North America after San Francisco's Chinatown.)

Lake Louise was discovered in 1882 and named Emerald Lake. It was renamed in 1884 after Princess Louise Caroline Alberta, from whom our province also gets its name. The hamlet which developed there was originally called Holt City (1883) and then Laggan (1883-1914) and in 1916 its name was officially changed to match that of the lake.

Nanton, south of Calgary, is famous for its spring water, which comes from the Big Spring in the Porcupine Hills (10 kilometres to the west). There is a big tap right along Highway 2 in town, where weary travellers can refresh themselves.

At the time I was there the tap had not yet been turned on for the summer.

South Moraine Lake and the Valley of the Ten Peaks, located 13 kilometres east of the Lake Louise access road, is pictured on the Canadian $20 bill.

Compare the photo here with the picture on the back of a $20 bill. If there are any differences other than the tree in the foreground, send your bill to me and I will take care of it.

The first inland lighthouse between the West Coast and the Great Lakes was officially opened on August 7, 1988 at Sylvan Lake, west of Red Deer. It was a joint project of the town of Sylvan Lake, Sylvan Lake Marina and Sylvan Lake Regional Sailing Club. It stands 17 metres in height and among the electronics to be installed is a wind-speed indicator and a voice-activated

computer that will tell callers wind-speed and direction, updating every fifteen minutes.

A 90-million-ton rock slide in 1903 wiped out most of the town of Frank. The Frank Slide Interpretive Centre, located on the west end of the slide, which came down Turtle Mountain, contains the story of the slide and the early history of the area.

At 1540 metres, Lake Louise is the highest town in Canada.

Crystal Village at Pincher Creek is a set of thirteen buildings made by hand, from 200,000 insulators and 900 crossarms from telephone lines.

Sylvan Lake was originally called Methy Lake, then Swan Lake, then Snake Lake, before acquiring its present name. The original settlers in

Sylvan Lake lighthouse

Crystal village and its owner/builder, Bastian (Boss) Zoeteman.

this area were from Michigan and they were followed by Finnish and Russian immigrants in the early 1900s. Since 1904 it has become a well known summer resort.

The locality of Wood River is not located on, or near a river, but rather was named after a place of the same name in Nebraska, U.S.A.

In 1978 the towns of Blairmore and Coleman, the villages of Bellevue and Frank, and Improvement District No. 5 were combined to form the municipality of Crowsnest Pass.

Southeastern

Airways, Alberta, received its name when it was surveyed from the air along a proposed railway line from Alliance, Alberta, to Unity, Saskatchewan. The rail line was never laid through the locality nor was there an airport built there.

Bow Island is the town that was once literally on the skids. In depression years, some settlers put their houses on skids so they could move away.

In April of 1964 the town of Cardston, Alberta, received international fame when it enacted By-law No. 1113 under Section 306 of Alberta's Town and Village Act. This by-law prohibited the advertising of tobacco products within the town, by way of " . . . signs, billboards, placards, banners and handbills."

Cardston has no liquor outlets, nor will it allow any, as the town wishes to uphold high moral standards. The citizens have recently developed a tourism action plan, which will include publicizing the place as a "dry" town.

The last official act of the administration of the North-West Territories, Alberta District, was to incorporate the town of Claresholm. That was on August 31, 1905. The following day, Alberta became a province of the Dominion of Canada.

The site of the city of Drumheller was first settled by Thomas Greentree in 1902. Shortly afterward Samuel Drumheller came along and helped develop the townsite. These two gentlemen agreed the toss of a coin would be the determining factor in naming the community.

In the area between Medicine Hat and Lethbridge lies Legend Lake. It received its name from Indian legends which told of a great fish in the lake that was known to swallow canoes along with their inhabitants.

The Handhills are about 35 kilometres west of Hanna, and are the second highest point of land between the Rocky Mountains and the east coast. They acquired this name when it was noted that they form the shape of a human hand.

Langdon was named after Mr. Langdon of the C.P. Railway construction firm of Langdon and Shepard. Established in 1883 as one of two major rail stops between Medicine Hat and Calgary, its boom period was from 1904 to 1910. It was called the good luck town in 1908, and a sign was put up that year featuring a horseshoe emblem. The "good luck town" has actually flooded out twice, as it is located in a wide valley. It now has raised wooden boardwalks, with boat rings imbedded in them, in case of future floods.

Lethbridge averages more hours of sunshine per year than any other place in Canada.

Lloydminster is the only city in Canada located in two provinces. The main street of the city sits on the Alberta/Saskatchewan border. The population is: Alberta side - 10,201; Saskatchewan side - 7,115; total - 17,316.

Stevenson Hall Block

The oldest building in Red Deer is the Stevensen Hall Block, built in 1890 by Mr. I. Stevensen. It has served as Red Deer's first law office, first land titles office, first bank, first service station and was the first site for city council meetings.

The song *Prairie Rose* was inspired by the picturesque community of Rosebud. This, in turn, produced the idea for Alberta's floral emblem and the motto "Wild Rose Country."

Taber, Alberta is well known for the sweetness of its corn.

Main Street in Lloydminster

ALBERTA PLACE NAMES QUIZ

Match the clues below with the appropriate names of
Alberta communities in the second column.

1.	Animal's home	Nojack
2.	Barber's challenge	Dunmore
3.	Breakfast	Canmore
4.	Yes, Bill	Gift Lake
5.	Bumpy drive up	Duchess
6.	...............Oil	Stand Off
7.	Chinese cooking	Entrance
8.	Connecting agreement	Beaverlodge
9.	Dirty appendage	Foremost
10.	Overdid it	Legal
11.	Doorway	Cereal
12.	Duke's wife	Champion
13.	Embarrassed venison	Reno
14.	Exaggerating water	Alliance
15.	Ex-service person	North Star
16.	First and	Michichi
17.	Flat above	Fairview
18.	.... of speech.	Castor
19.	Guiding light	Red Deer
20.	Great middle	Big Valley
21.	Higher education	Viking
22.	Large long depression	Bonanza
23.	Lawful	Hairy Hill
24.	Lucky strike	Consort
25.	Monarch's day	Milk River
26.	No clouds	Bragg Creek
27.	No winner	Coronation
28.	Noisy pond	Blackfoot
29.	Pleasant to look at	Bluesky
30.	Whitewater	Carstairs
31.	Prescription headgear	Grand Centre
32.	............, Nevada	High Level
33.	Royal companion	Redcliff
34.	Scandinavian pirate	Calling Lake
35.	The best	Veteran
36.	Blue mountain	College Heights
37.	Place with lots of tins	Longview
38.	Water of presents	Woking
39.	Short peek	Medicine Hat
40.	Your what?	Freedom

All names taken from Alberta Government *Travel Alberta* roadmaps.

See if you can answer these questions:

41. Who is Mount Lougheed named after?
42. Where and what is pictured on the reverse side of a Canadian $20 dollar bill?
43. What is the highest point of land in Alberta?
44. Where is the lowest point of land in Alberta?
45. Where are the Saskatchewan and Athabasca glaciers located?
46. What two Alberta cities share a common border?
47. Who was the only Albertan to be granted knighthood?

On the Yellowhead Highway approximately 70-75 kilometres west of Edmonton you may see signs with the following names.

48. Yo Wo Ch As - what is the origin of this name?

49. He Ho Ha - what does this name mean?

50. Kokomoko - what is the origin of this name?

Answers for this quiz can be found in the back of the book.

BUSINESS AND INDUSTRY

The principal industries of Alberta are: petroleum, agriculture, tourism, forestry and manufacturing.

Over 90 per cent of the water supply for the prairie provinces of Canada comes from Alberta.

Northern Alberta was commercially developed before southern Alberta. The north was opened up by the fur traders in the latter half of the 1700s and the south was opened up by missionaries who established churches and schools during the mid-1800s.

Alberta's unemployment went up 234.8% in the years of 1980 to 1984. This was the highest rate in Canada for that period. (The next closest was B.C. at 136.7% in the same period.)

Approximately 66% of Canada's workforce is in Ontario and Quebec. About 20% are in Alberta and B.C. and 14% are in the rest of Canada. In 1984 about 813,100 were employed in Alberta with average weekly earnings of $439.27. (Nationally the number employed was 8,653,600 with earnings of $405.13 weekly).

Average family income in Alberta for the year 1987 was $44,388. Ontario was highest at $48,967, Alberta second, and Newfoundland was lowest at $33,710. (These figures were released by Statistics Canada in December of 1988.)

EMPLOYMENT IN ALBERTA

Year	Employed	Unemployed
1927	1,271,000	125,000
1976	838,000	35,000
1980	1,078,000	42,000
1984	1,114,000	140,000

Percentage Change

Years	Employed	Unemployed
1976 - 80	28.6	21.3
1980 - 84	3.3	234.8

For the year ending March 31, 1988, Alberta's gross provincial revenue was $11.3 billion and its total expenditures was $12.68 billion.

Among Canada's 15 major cities during the 1980s, Calgary had the lowest rate of inflation at 36.8 per cent. Edmonton and Charlottetown tied for second lowest at 38.1 and Toronto was the highest at 52.8 per cent.

For 1988 Alberta's Gross Domestic Product (GDP) was estimated at $61 billion. (Alberta's GDP is larger than that of some countries in the world.)

The estimated size of Alberta's Heritage Trust Fund at the end of fiscal year March 31, 1988 was $12.5 billion.

About 75% of Alberta's exports go to the United States. In 1988 this represented a dollar value of $13.5 billion.

The Alberta government has put more money per capita into science than any other province.

The Edmonton Convention Centre is home to the Junior Achievement of Northern Alberta Business Hall of Fame.

The first Treasury Branch opened in Alberta in Rocky Mountain House on September 29, 1938. The following day five other branches were officially opened, in Andrew, Killam, St. Paul, Grande Prairie and Edmonton.

BUSINESS MISCELLANEOUS

The first store was opened in Alberta in 1778. It was a trading post, built by Peter Pond of Montreal, and was situated about 30 miles from Lake Athabasca on the Athabasca River.

A store in Lundbreck claims to be the oldest shopping centre in the West.

There are no retail sales taxes in Alberta, but there is a 5% room tax on all hotel and motel rooms.

In percentage of total retail sales, Alberta was fourth highest in Canada in 1984, after Ontario, Quebec and B.C. Per capita, Alberta was first in sales ($5,100) followed by Ontario ($4,800) and Nova Scotia ($4,600).

Saskatoon berries are very common throughout Alberta. Very few people have not eaten them in one way or another: from the bush, or in pies, jams, preserves, etc. In November, 1986, the Lewis Brothers Winery opened in Grande Prairie, producing such wines as Nouveau Saskatoon and Wild Rose Mead. It is the first such winery in Canada. (Saskatoon berries derive their name from the Cree Indian word "Mis-sask-quah-too-min.")

The Andrew Wolf Wine Cellars in Stony Plain use 100-year-old oak casks to age wine.

One of the oldest potteries in Alberta is the Beaver Flats Pottery, located approximately 10 kilometres west of Leslieville. This is the only privately owned studio combining facilities for the production of pottery and blown glass in Canada.

Medalta Potteries in Medicine Hat was, at one time, the best known pottery in Canada. It opened in 1912 and shut down in 1960. In 1976 Medalta became the first Provincial Industrial Historic Site in Alberta and in 1985 was designated as a National Historic Site.

The Custom Woollen Mill, located about 25 kilometres east of Carstairs, is the only one of its kind in western Canada. Some of their complex machines, run by specially trained employees, were designed in 1856.

Total value of all construction work in Alberta in 1987 was $10,110,200,000.

Manulife Place in Edmonton was declared Canada's Building of the Year by BOMA (Building Owners and Managers Association) during their national awards program. They took first place in the "over 500,000 square feet" category. The manager of the building's administration office says this is " . . . like winning the heavy-weight class in boxing."

The Calgary Tower is one of the tallest in North America. It is 190.8 metres high and the elevator ride to the

Manulife building, Edmonton

observation deck takes 63 seconds. Also located at the top is a revolving dining room. It was built in 1967.

The Petro-Canada Centre in Calgary is the tallest building in western Canada and the tallest in Canada outside of Toronto. The building has two retail floors, 50 floors of office space, and, at the top, three floors of mechanical space. From the street level it is 215 metres high. It is designed for a working population of about 5,000 and is serviced by a total of 49 elevators. Below ground there are four levels of parking space.

Petro-Canada building, Calgary

The Alamo Hotel in Suffield in 1914 had " . . . a bar 40 feet long and unique square flush toilets."

It was estimated that Alberta had almost 22 million visitors in 1988 as a result of the Winter Olympics, held in Calgary early in the year, and the provincial "Take an Alberta Break" campaign that was publicized mainly in B.C., Saskatchewan, Washington and Montana. Tourism in Alberta generates revenues of about $2.3 billion annually, resulting in approximately 75,000 full-time jobs.

On July 22, 1988, the largest seating-capacity theatre complex in Canada was opened at Edmonton's Eaton Centre. The Cineplex Odeon has nine

The Calgary Tower

large, wide-screen, state-of-the-art cinemas, with a total seating capacity of 3,400.

The largest boot in the world is about four stories high, cost about a quarter of a million dollars, and took 2,000 man hours to build. It is located at Western Boot Factory in Edmonton and is slated for the next Guinness Book of World Records.

In 1987, Albertans spent almost $720 million gambling on bingos, casinos, lotteries and raffles. (This figure does not include the racetracks.)

The top western Canadian winners ever were Ron and Val Taylor of Killam, Alberta, who won $10,372,326.70 in 1989. The second largest lottery jackpot ever won in Alberta was $10 million, won by three Calgary men, Ken Brown, Wing Gee and Terry Johnston, on December 23, 1989. Of the top ten lottery winners in western Canada, four were from Alberta and three of these are from Edmonton.

In the Lotto 6/49, there are 13,983,816 different six-digit combinations.

In the Lotto 6/36, there are 1,947,792 different six-digit combinations.

About half of Alberta's commercial fishing catch is whitefish.

In 1984 Alberta produced a total of 31,058.9 gigawatt hours of electricity, mostly by conventional steam generating.

Two thirds of the electrical energy consumed in Alberta is supplied by TransAlta Utilities, serving approximately 600,000 customers (1,500,000 people).

The Big Horn Dam

The Big Horn Dam is one of the largest earth-filled dams in western Canada and electricity is generated here for Edmonton and the surrounding areas.

On April 1, 1984, because of environmental concerns, the government of Alberta created the Alberta Special Waste Management System and constructed a facility capable of neutralizing hazardous waste materials. Special waste collection days, called Toxic Round-ups, have been organized in individual communities and wastes collected are properly packaged and shipped to one of the most advanced waste treatment plants in the world, located at Swan Hills. For more information call 1-800-252-9300 or if in Edmonton, 427-9300.

OIL AND NATURAL GAS

The petroleum industry in Alberta had its beginning in 1886 when John Kootenai Brown started selling oil he had skimmed from Cameron Creek in the Waterton district of southeastern Alberta, for $1 per gallon.

In 1930, Premier Brownley obtained exclusive ownership of Alberta's natural resources, including oil, for the government of Alberta.

Alberta owns the largest deposits of natural gas and oil in the country.

The natural gas industry in Alberta dates from discoveries near Medicine Hat in 1885.

The Alberta oil sands consist of four huge underground deposits of water-saturated sand, bitumen and clay. Over a trillion barrels of heavy bitumen lie under the earth's surface in the regions of Peace River, Wabaska, Cold Lake and Athabasca Regions.

The total mineral production in Alberta in 1984 had a value of $25,963,735,000. This is by far the highest provincial figure in Canada; the second highest was Ontario's at $4,493,725,000.

Petroleum, natural gas and their by-products accounted for over 90% of Alberta's mineral production, by value, in 1986.

Royalties from oil and gas resources, paid to the government of Alberta for the year that ended March 31, 1988, were $2.6 billion.

In 1984 Alberta produced 90% of the total of Canadian crude oil, natural gas and natural gas by-products.

There are about 17,000 producing oil wells in Alberta.

Alberta has over 100,000 kilometres of pipeline carrying oil and gas to both internal and external markets.

Oil City was Alberta's first producing oil well. It is marked by an historical cairn on the Akamina Parkway, where there is a short path to some building foundations, all that is left of the town. This was actually the first oil well in western Canada. It was brought in by the Rocky Mountain Development Company when they struck oil at 1,024 ft. (312 m) in 1902. Production commenced at 300 barrels per day but by 1904 the well was dry. Although insignificant by today's standards, the discovery of this well prompted the search which led to the discovery of the Turner Valley oil field, which was the first major oil and gas field in the British Commonwealth. Oil City is now known as the city that never was.

Oil was discovered in the Turner Valley in 1914 at the site of the Dingman No. 1 oil well. The area

One of the larger oil well pumping systems.

rapidly became the centre of Alberta's oil industry, and remained in that role for many years. R.A. Brown was at the forefront of the race to develop this resource and he subsequently became known as the father of Alberta's modern day oil industry. In its early years this was Canada's greatest oil producing district.

Gateway Park, just south of Edmonton on the Calgary Trail (Highway 2), features the Imperial Leduc No. 1 Oil Derrick and Interpretive Centre, which commemorates the oil strike near Leduc on February 13, 1947. The displays were set up to honour the pioneers of oil exploration.

The Leduc oil field was discovered in the geological formation known as the Devonian. The nearby town of Devon is named after this formation.

The town of Drayton Valley is situated in the heart of the largest oil field, by area, in the nation.

Fort McMurray is home of the world's largest known oil deposit — the world-

famous tar sands. Also the world's first oil mine is working here.

The Alberta Oil Sands Technology and Research Authority, an Alberta Crown Corporation, operates one of the largest research and development programs in Canada.

One of the by-products of the oil sands processing plants is the metal vanadium. It is used as a metal hardening agent and Fort McMurray is the only place in Canada where it is obtained.

The world's largest hydraulic excavator went into service on January 2, 1989 on the oil sands at Fort McMurray. It was assembled by Wajax Industries Mining Division of Edmonton. It has a total service weight of 600 metric tonnes and the shovel has a 26 cubic metre capacity.

The world's largest hydraulic excavator

It takes approximately 22 m³ of water to refine one cubic metre of petroleum.

The Peter Lougheed Bridge at Fort McMurray is called the bridge to nowhere, because it was built to lead to the Alsands oil sands plant, which wasn't constructed after all.

Oil City Cairn

Imperial Leduc No. 1 Oil Derrick

Albertans pay no provincial gasoline sales tax.

The book *Kangaroo Rats and Rattlesnakes*, published by CFB Suffield, states "There is an operating gas well in Suffield that has been providing fuel since the turn of the century."

The first gas well site in Lloydminster is now marked by a cairn in Weaver Park.

The largest natural gas field in North America is located just west of Grande Prairie.

Drilling activity in Alberta during 1988 showed an increase of 24.5% over 1987. There were 6,378 wells drilled in Alberta which made up 71.8% of the total wells drilled in Canada. The overall success rate for drilling is about 74 per cent.

During the mid-1970s, energy resource prices were such that Alberta benefited enormously. The huge surpluses being realized caused the government to create the Alberta Heritage Savings Trust Fund. The purpose of the fund is to " . . . provide financial resources for periods when resource income declines, to strengthen and diversify the provincial economy, and to undertake special capital projects."

COAL

The first coal mine in Alberta was on the west bank of the Oldman River in 1872. The federal mine in Lethbridge now occupies this site.

Alberta has approximately 80 per cent of the known coal reserves in Canada.

The energy content of Alberta's coal reserves is equal to that of the oil sands and heavy oil reserves combined.

Of all the power produced in Alberta in 1986, 91.6% of it was the result of coal-fired generating. By 1989 this figure reached 95 per cent.

Sundance Power Plant

Coal in Alberta is cleaner than coal in other parts of the country because of its low sulphur content; thus, electricity generated from coal in Alberta is relatively pollution free.

The largest coal-fired generating station in Alberta is the Sundance Power Plant on Wabamun Lake. Owned by TransAlta Utilities, it has the capacity to supply almost half of Alberta's electrical energy requirements. Located on the south shore of Wabamun Lake, it uses about 8.5 million tonnes of coal per year.

TransAlta Utilities produces 24% of all the coal mined in Canada, (over 14 million tonnes per year), and over 50% of all coal mined in Alberta. Their two main mines, the Whitewood and Highvale, have coal reserves of 724 million tonnes.

The Genesee Coal Mine officially began production on December 14, 1988. It is a joint venture between Fording Coal Ltd. and Edmonton Power. The coal reserves in the mine are estimated at over 270 million tonnes, and the rate of extraction will be about 1.5 million tonnes per year, based on current consumption rates and estimated future needs.

Fording Coal Ltd. is mining coal for the Genesee Generating Station, which began generating electricity for the Alberta Inter-connected System in October, 1989. The dragline for this mining project took over a year to assemble. The giant crane, which moves on huge walking "shoes" at about 2 metres per minute, can dig to a maximum depth of 46 metres, and has a bucket capacity of 50 cubic metres. The station is capable of generating 400 megawatts of electricity — enough to meet the needs of a quarter of a million people.

The Rosedale Suspension Bridge is a unique foot bridge that was built originally by coal miners in 1931, to replace an old cable trolley system. It was used by the coal miners going to, or coming from work at the Star Mine, and at that time had no side barriers. The structure has been rebuilt and upgraded for the safety of the traffic it carries today — mainly sightseers.

The Forestburg Collieries & Paintearth Mine together make up a strip mining operation, which uses one of the largest draglines in the world. The Marion 8200 walking dragline has a working weight of 4175 tons, and a 52-cubic-metre bucket.

Rosedale Suspension Bridge

The longest continuous conveyor belt in Alberta is 11.2 kilometres long. It is owned and operated by the Obed Mountain Coal Company near Obed Summit east of Hinton. The belt transports coal from the mine to the rail loading facilities and, when full, it carries 500 tonnes and takes about 45 minutes to complete the trip. The belt is raised in eight places along its length to allow for animal crossings.

The longest conveyor belt in Alberta.

There have been 138 registered coal mines in the Drumheller area.

It takes approximately 1.36 kg (3 lb.) of coal to produce the electricity required to light a 100-watt bulb for 24 hours.

MINING DISASTERS

At the mining town of Frank, in 1903, 90 million tons of rock was deposited in the valley, taking up two square miles in 100 seconds, to a depth of 100 feet. Only part of the town was buried but it is estimated over 70 people lost their lives.

One of the worst mining disasters in Canada occurred on June 19, 1914, at the Hillcrest Coal and Coke Companies mine in the Crowsnest Pass area of Alberta. An explosion took the lives of 189 miners.

This sign is found at the Hillcrest Cemetery.

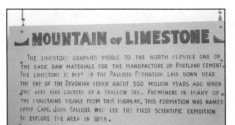

OTHER MINES

Besides coal, oil and natural gas, Alberta produces salt, sodium sulphate, peat moss, and construction minerals such as limestone, sand, clay and gypsum. Some gold and other metallics are mined here. So are low-grade iron ore and uranium, in the Lake Athabasca region. Alberta is also the largest sulphur producer in the world.

The Canadian Salt Company at Lindberg produces 350,000 kilograms of salt per day. The salt is mined 760 metres below the surface and brought up in solution form, and the reserves in this mine are enough to supply Canada's needs for at least the next 2,000 years.

Approximately three kilometres west and 11 kilometres south of Metiskow is the plant of Froncana Minerals which mines natural sodium sulphate deposits. The higher grade material is used for detergents and the lower grade is sent to pulp mills to be used for bleaching.

The Canadian Salt Company plant at Lindberg.

Recent discoveries indicate that the Lost Lemon Gold Mine may be in the Crowsnest Pass area.

FORESTRY

Over half of Canada is covered by forests and 10 per cent of the world's forest products comes from Canada. Alberta's forest industry contributes about $900 million annually to the provincial economy. This industry directly employs about 9,000 workers and indirectly employs another 20,000.

Projections for 1989 to 1992 indicated that Alberta's forest industry development would represent new investment of $3.4 billion.

In an effort to protect unique or representative ecosystems, wildlife habitats and recreation areas, and sensitive environments, over 27% of Alberta's forests has been off limits for resource development activities.

The largest producer of softwoods in Alberta is the Canfor Sawmill complex at High Level. The fully computerized mill uses 200 truckloads of lumber per day.

The first pulp mill in Alberta is owned by Weldwood, and was opened at Hinton in 1957 by Champion Forest

Products Ltd. The two other pulp mills in Alberta are in Grande Prairie and Whitecourt, and are owned by Proctor and Gamble and Millar Western respectively.

Alberta's forest industry reforested about 30,800 hectares of woodlands in 1987.

The first buildings in Alberta to be erected with sawn lumber were at Lac La Biche.

Approximately 100 kilometres southwest of Calgary, in the Beehive Natural Area, is a forest that is over 1,000 years old, with individual trees over 300 years old.

The Ancient Forest of the Columbia Icefield, located behind the Icefield Centre, has been granted Zone One - Special Preservation status by the Alberta government. This is the highest level of protection available from the province. This small section of Engelmann spruce is over 700 years old. The trees are tiny compared to their cousins on the west coast, the Sitka spruce, because they have been stunted by barren soil and severe weather conditions. Some of these trees were over 200 years old when Columbus discovered America.

In 1986, as a tribute to the forests of the nation, the local Forest Service Branch in Whitecourt invited each province in Canada to send two of its native trees to the town, where they were planted along the highway.

One of the very few places in Canada where Burmis trees grow is along Highway 3 in the Lundbreck-Burmis area. These trees are a favorite subject of photographers.

Burmis tree

The average tree produces 453,000 toothpicks according to researcher Bruce Lovatt (reported in the *Edmonton Sun* by columnist Donna Marie Artuso).

Forests harbour about half of all Earth's living organic matter. One third is in the oceans, and the rest can be found in croplands and grass areas.

An acre of managed, healthy second-growth forest can consume 5 to 6 tons of carbon dioxide a year, and can release about 4 tons of fresh oxygen. It also grows about 4 tons of new wood per year during the growing cycle.

Water makes up over 80% of a tree's total living weight.

AGRICULTURE

The first wheat grown in Alberta was at Lac La Biche.

The Cochrane Ranch was established in 1878 by, and named after, Senator M.H. Cochrane (1823-1903). In 1881 the ranch was incorporated as the Cochrane Ranch Company, and it was the first of the big ranches of the West (see also provincial parks section).

The oldest existing flour mill in Alberta was declared a provincial historic site in 1979. The Ritchie Mill was built in 1893. It is on Saskatchewan Drive in Edmonton.

In 1901 William Fairfield, operating a model farm south of Lethbridge for the Canadian North West Irrigation Company, recognized the reason local soils would not produce alfalfa. He imported a few pounds of Rhizobium bacteria-rich soil from Wyoming's alfalfa-rich area, and spread it around his farm, thus inoculating the soil. Soil from here was later spread throughout other areas.

The Brooks Aqueduct was called an engineering miracle for its time. Built in 1914, this cement waterway carried 650 cubic feet of water per second, at heights of up to 60 feet above ground, for two miles. Plans are underway to make the aqueduct an historical monument. The structure is still there but an earth-lined channel now serves as the aqueduct for that area. See provincial parks section for more information.

The Alberta Wheat Pool was formed in 1923 by the United Farmers of Alberta (UFA) after they won the provincial election in 1921.

The first world prize ever presented for wheat was won by Herman Trelle of the Wembley area in 1927.

The Ritchie Flour Mill

The Northern Alberta Dairy Pool (NADP) was formed in 1928.

The federal government passed the Prairie Farm Rehabilitation Act in 1935 to prevent the prairies from eroding into deserts. Included in the plans were strip farming, shelter belts, grass seeding and new methods of cultivation.

The Brooks Aqueduct

Alberta is one of the few places in the world that is "rat free." A rat colony was found in 1950 on a farm in southern Alberta near the Saskatchewan border, but an intensive control program soon eliminated the rodents.

Of the 293,000 farms in Canada, 57,777 of them are in Alberta, and their average size is 354 hectares.

It takes approximately 13 tons of wood to make one ton of paper.

The primary commodity produced in Alberta is cattle and calves.

Farms have legal addresses just like houses in a city. Here is an example: NW12 35 13 W4. This farm is located on the northwest quarter of section 12 in Township 35 on Range 13 west of the 4th meridian. Townships begin at one at the Canadian - U.S. border and the numbers get larger as they go north. Meridian 4 lies along the Alberta - Saskatchewan border. The numbering of ranges begins at 1 and gets larger as you travel west.

Almost 50% of the Canadian oat crop is produced in Alberta.

Many world wheat champions have come from the Beiseker - Drumheller area.

Although Alberta has only 9.2% of Canada's population, it produces about 20% of the nation's food.

Alberta accounted for 10% of Canada's chicken production in 1984.

Spruce Meadows, located just south of Calgary, is known as the Equestrian Centre of North America.

Canada's largest pony ranch is the Graham Ranche at East Coulee, Alberta.

Of some 37 agricultural research stations in Canada outside of Ottawa, the largest is the Lethbridge Agricultural Centre. It consists of 440 hectares of field plots and livestock facilities and 18,280 hectares at three substations.

The first irrigation dam built in Alberta is at Bassano and it is still in use. The Bassano dam and irrigation system now has 4,506 kilometres of canals providing water for 98,800 hectares of land, two towns, three villages and four hamlets.

The Peace River region of northwestern Alberta contains the worlds most northerly grain-growing area.

The latest concept in grain storage was initiated at the town of Magrath a few years ago. It is called a buffalo-sloped elevator and its design is rather unusual. With the success of this design, similar elevators were built in Vegreville and Fort Saskatchewan. The Buffalo 2000, a recent design, has now been used in Boyle, Foremost and Lyalta. The technology of these elevators has been exported to other parts of the world including Brazil.

The E.P. Ranch west of High River was owned for 42 years by H.R.H. Edward VIII.

The first known outbreak in Canada of Potomac Horse Fever occurred in Alberta's Delburne area in 1988. Until then it had been known only in the U.S. where it was first recognized in 1979. This sometimes fatal disease of horses has symptoms of high temperature, depression, loss of appetite and diarrhea.

The largest ice cream sundae in the world was put together by Palm Dairies Ltd., in celebration of its 60th birthday. The sundae consisted of 20,110 kg ice cream, 4,360 kg topping, 90 kg whipped cream, 50 kg peanuts and 50 kg cherries. It was built in the Edmonton Convention Centre, during Edmonton's Klondike Days on July 24, 1988, and verified by a representative of the Guinness Book of World Records.

The Calgary Italian Bakery, sponsored

Buffalo sloped elevator at Magrath.

by the Southern Alberta Bakers Association, created the largest loaf of bread ever baked on July 7, 1986. It measured 2.75 metres by 1.5 metres and weighed 1,384 kg.

The Bassano Dam

GARDENS

Edmonton's Muttart Conservatory is a set of four pyramid-shaped glass structures containing permanent displays of plant life of arid, tropical and temperate climates, and one changing display.

The Calgary Devonian Gardens are located in a one-hectare indoor park on the fourth level of the Toronto Dominion Square, which is between 2nd Street & 3rd Street and 7th Avenue & 8th Avenue N.W. in Calgary. Featured are some 20,000 sub-tropical plants, including almost 140 tropical and local varieties, set among 1.6 kilometres of pathways, pools, fountains, a waterfall and bridges.

The Nikka Yuko Japanese Garden in Lethbridge was constructed in 1967 as a centennial project to honour the Japanese Canadians who were interned here during World War II. Doctor Tadashi Kubo, of Osaka, designed the garden using techniques over 1,000 years old. All the structures within the garden were built in Japan and later assembled in Lethbridge. They are constructed without nails or bolts, from

Muttart Gardens, Edmonton

Devonian Gardens, Calgary

knot-free wood chosen for the straightness of its grain. Only water, rocks, and green shrubs were used, because Japanese gardens were originally used for meditation purposes and it was believed at that time that flowers would be distracting.

Other outstanding gardens in Alberta include the Galt Gardens in Lethbridge and the Sicks Brewery Garden, also in Lethbridge.

Some of the largest greenhouse operations in Alberta are at Oyen.

SERVICES

EDUCATION

The first schools in Alberta were started by missionaries in the mid-nineteenth century and were usually conducted in the place of worship.

Edmonton's first schoolhouse, located on Heritage Trail, was built in 1881.

Alberta has four universities: the University of Alberta (U of A) in Edmonton, the University of Calgary (U of C), the University of Lethbridge (U of L), and the Athabasca University.

The University of Alberta opened its doors in October of 1908 and by 1910 had 140 students, studying Arts and Applied Science.

Dr. A.C. Rutherford, the first premier of Alberta, was instrumental in the founding of the University of Alberta.

The University of Alberta is Canada's second largest university with over 25,000 students and a staff of 8,000.

The University of Calgary became a fully autonomous university in 1966 and now has 16 faculties with over 17,000 full-time students and another 5,000 part-time.

Other than the four universities in Alberta there are the Northern Alberta Institute of Technology in Edmonton and the Southern Alberta Institute of

EDUCATIONAL FACILITIES 1985/86

1585 public and separate schools (grades 1-12)
11 public colleges
3 technical institutes
4 universities
4 vocational centres
2 specialized schools
4 private colleges
6 hospital based schools of nursing

Technology in Calgary. There are also ten public colleges in Alberta.

The first public junior college established in Canada was the Lethbridge Community College. It has a 58-hectare campus.

Canada's only interprovincial college is Lakeland College at Vermilion. It was founded in 1913 as an agricultural school.

The first branch of the International High School of Marine Sciences of Ogasa, Japan, is located in Spruce Grove, Alberta.

The Banff Centre School of Fine Arts is an internationally known school for training young professionals in the arts.

Alberta, Saskatchewan and Ontario are the only three provinces of Canada which, by legislation, allow the establishment of separate schools.

The only provincial governments in Canada to operate their own educational TV networks are Alberta, British Columbia, Ontario and Quebec.

Students from Barrhead School District won the provincial championship on the TV show "Reach for the Top" four times, and were the first team to win the national championship.

Outside of the government's system of school jurisdictions, there are 117 private schools which are operated by societies. This means their board members are not elected by the general public or the public at large.

MEDICINE

RELIGION

The first white baby was born in Alberta in the winter of 1809-10 at Fort Edmonton. The mother, Marie-Anne Lagemodière (née Gaboury), was the first white woman in permanent residence in Alberta.

Edmonton was the first municipality in Alberta to establish its own Board of Health, in 1892.

According to the 1988 Alberta Touring Guide, the first municipal hospital built in the British Commonwealth was at Mannville, Alberta. However, according to a sign in Riverside Park, Medicine Hat, "The first municipal hospital in the North-West Territories and the only medical institution between Winnipeg and the West Coast was built in 1889 in Medicine Hat."

The Red Cross began operating in Alberta on May 6, 1914.

The first Hospital District in Alberta was created in 1918.

In 1928 a diptheria epidemic broke out in the Fort Vermilion area. Heroic efforts by men like "Wop" May and Dick Horner to fly in serum, despite open cockpit planes and -30°F temperatures, became well known and brought the importance of the bush plane to the attention of the world.

Alberta had, as of March 1986: 123 public hospitals; 2 federal general hospitals; 2 mental health hospitals; 44 auxiliary hospitals; and 87 nursing homes.

There are more than 4,000 doctors in Alberta.

There are more than 1,000 dentists in Alberta.

The first straw church built in Canada is located northeast of Grande Prairie and Teepee Creek. This unusual building, at first glance, does not appear to be any different than any other building. It is actually made of bales of hay on a concrete foundation and with a wooden frame. The walls are about 0.6 metres (2 ft.) thick. On the outside the hay was covered with chicken wire and then stuccoed. It was originally built in 1954 under the direction of Father Richard Dale. It was recently purchased and restored by the Bad Heart Cultural Association. To get there from Teepee Creek go approximately 1.5 kilometres east, 3 kilometres north, 6.8 kilometres east and 9.3 kilometres north. For more information or a tour booking phone 568-4279, 568-2971 or 568-4047.

The Straw Church

The hamlet of Dickson, located in northwestern Alberta, is home to Canada's first Danish Lutheran congregation.

In 1840 methodist Robert Rundle was the first missionary to establish a permanent place of worship in Alberta. The second was the Roman Catholic Mission established by Father Jean-Baptiste Thibault, O.M.I., in 1843 at Lac Ste. Anne, west of Edmonton.

In early August of every year, several thousand people gather at Lac Ste. Anne for the feast of Ste. Anne, an annual celebration marking the birthday of the Virgin Mary's mother.

Two communities in Alberta are named for Father Albert Lacombe: the city of St. Albert (named after Father Lacombe's patron saint) and the town of Lacombe. He also established the first site of Brosseau as St. Paul de Cris.

Father Albert Lacombe monument, St. Albert

A plaque in the Edmonton Convention Centre reads "On this site the first services of the Presbyterian Church were held Nov. 1881 - Nov. 1882. Minister Rev. Andrew B. Baird."

On February 24, 1928, the Edmonton Presbytery voted that women ministers and the admission of women in all the church courts would be permitted.

Dove of Peace

Pope John Paul II paid a visit to Namao, of central Alberta, in September 1984. He conducted a mass under a specially built 24-foot-high fiberglass canopy shaped to represent the dove of peace. It was then taken apart and it lay on the grounds of the Muttart Conservatory in Edmonton until the fall of 1988. Fundraising efforts resurrected the Dove and it was officially dedicated on October 30, 1988, by Edmonton Mayor Terry Cavanaugh. The site contains a time capsule that will be opened in 100 years. An ongoing fundraising program will be conducted to pay for landscaping and maintenance costs.

The first Doukhobor settlement in Alberta was in the southwest near Cowley in 1915 when a group of about 300, belonging to the Christian Community of Universal Brotherhood, moved here from British Columbia.

Millarville Christ Church

The Millarville Christ Church, 3 kilometres north and 6.5 kilometres east of Millarville in southwestern Alberta, is unusual because it was made of spruce logs placed in an upright position. It was built in 1897.

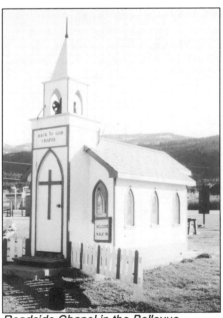

Roadside Chapel in the Bellevue - Hillcrest campground.

About 25 kilometres east of the B.C. border, in the Bellevue-Hillcrest campground, is a small road-side chapel which seats eight people and presents recorded sermons and music during the summer months.

The Mormon Temple at Cardston (in southeastern Alberta) is made of granite and was built by settlers belonging to the Church of Latter Day Saints. It is the only such temple in Canada.

Mormon Temple, Cardston

Gibbons Anglican Church

St. Mary's Catholic Church

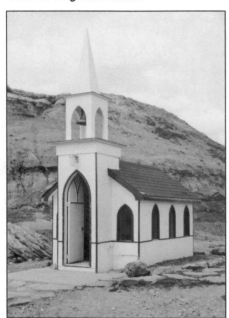

The World's Largest Little Church

The Gibbons Anglican Church, located at Gibbons in southeastern Alberta, was built in 1902 and its interior is built like a ship.

The World's Largest Little Church is situated along the Dinosaur Trail near Drumheller. It was dedicated in 1958 by Alberta's lieutenant-governor. The claim of this church is that it seats 10,000 people — six at a time. (This works out to filling up 1,666 times and then once with only four people.)

St. Mary's Catholic Church in Red Deer was the creation of Red Deer-born Métis architect Douglas Cardinal. At the time it was being built many citizens were outraged at the fortress-like design and predicted the closure of the church within a very short period. It was completed in 1968 and is today considered to be an architectural masterpiece. Mr. Cardinal is considered to be one of Canada's foremost architects, his latest masterpiece being Canada's Museum of Civilization in Ottawa.

COMMUNICATIONS

The first communication system into the prairies was the mail carried by the fur trappers between the trading posts and by canoes from the east. Today there are about 570 post offices in Alberta. This figure does not include sub-stations etc. Within this figure are 16 letter carrier offices. Altogether Canada Post serves about 250,000 residences and almost 29,000 business and commercial establishments in Alberta.

The first post office in Alberta was established by the North-West Mounted Police in Fort Macleod.

The first telegraph line reached Alberta in 1877.

There are nine daily newspapers in Alberta and about 127 weekly community newspapers.

TELEPHONES

Canadians talk more on the telephone than any other people. At last count Canada had over 16 million telephones — that's one phone for every 1.5 persons. We also make more long distance calls per capita than any other nation.

The first telephones in Alberta went into service on January 3, 1885, connecting the Edmonton telegraph office with a store in St. Albert.

The Bell Telephone Company started Alberta's first commercial telephone exchange in Calgary, in July 1887. There were forty connected by the system.

The first telephone company in Edmonton began in the 1890s. In 1905 the City of Edmonton bought the business from Alex Taylor. The city paid $17,000 for the company and named it the City of Edmonton Telephone Department. In 1940 they changed the name to City Telephone Systems. It acquired the name Edmonton Telephones in 1967, recently shortened to EdTel.

The first telephone operator in Edmonton was 13-year-old Jennie Lauder. She was hired on a part-time basis to operate Edmonton's first switchboard

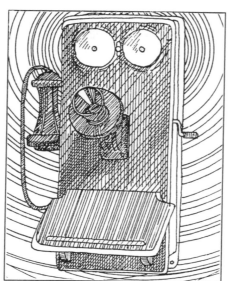

which was purchased for $200, secondhand, from the Montreal Fire Department.

Alberta was the first province in Canada to own and operate its own telephone system. Alberta Government Telephones took over existing systems in 1906 (except Edmonton Telephones).

The first color telephones in Alberta came in 1950.

In the 1950s, Canada's telephone companies began construction of the Trans-Canada Microwave System. This was completed through Alberta in 1957 and coast to coast service began July 1, 1958.

Alberta Government Telephones (AGT) has over 18.5 million kilometres of cables and microwave communication routes throughout Alberta (1987), and this includes approximately 1,210,052 telephone lines.

Alberta, on a per capita basis, had 78.7 telephones for every 100 persons in 1982 (the last available figures). This was the highest average in Canada; the national figure was 67.9 per 100 Canadians.

Vista 33 is located on the top floor of the Alberta Government Telephone Tower in downtown Edmonton (10020 - 100 Street). It is the Alberta Government Telephone's museum and

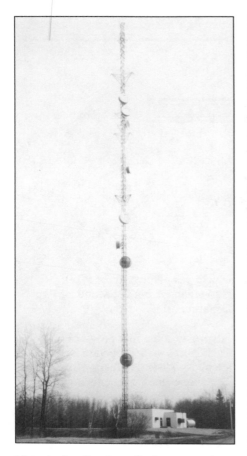

Edmonton Telephone Museum

historical collection of telecommunications equipment and artifacts. The walk-around gallery, at 118 metres above ground-level, provides excellent viewing of the city in every direction. It is well worth the modest admission charge.

The largest telephone museum in Canada is that of Edmonton Telephones located between 104th & 105th streets on 83rd Avenue in Edmonton.

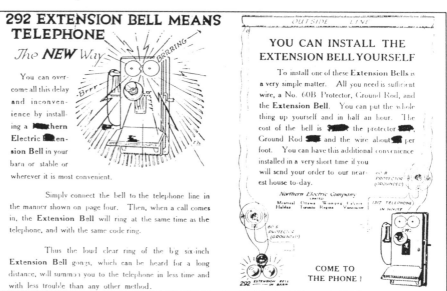

Before there were extension phones, there was the extension bell.

RADIO

The highlight of the Diamond Jubilee of Confederation celebrations being carried out across Canada was the first coast to coast radio network broadcast. The cost of these celebrations, which included crowds of 30,000 in Ottawa and 50,000 in Winnipeg, was $254,000. The date was July 1, 1927.

There are 65 AM radio stations in Alberta. This includes 15 CBC & 2 French language stations.

There are 58 FM radio stations in Alberta. This includes 14 CBC & 9 French language stations.

Even though Calgary's population is greater than Edmonton's, there are 10 AM radio stations and 10 FM stations in the capital city compared to 6 AM and 8 FM stations in Calgary.

At the Fourth Annual Industry Awards on March 11, 1989, Edmonton's 630 CHED received the title of Radio Station of the Year.

TELEVISION

Although television was actually invented in the 1920s, it was not until the late 1940s that television broadcasts were received in Alberta and these originated in the United States.

There are 127 television stations in Alberta.

POLITICS

The first premier of Alberta was Alexander Cameron Rutherford, who served from 1905 to 1910. In 1902, he was elected to the legislature of the North-West Territories, and in August of 1905 he became leader of the Alberta Liberal Association. The new lieutenant-governor asked him to help form the first Alberta government, which he did on September 2, 1905. On November 9th, he and his party won the first provincial election, taking 23 out of the 25 seats. As well as being premier, Rutherford served as provincial treasurer and minister of education. R.B. Bennett, leader of the Conservative opposition, moved on to become prime minister from 1930 to 1935.

The first legislature of Alberta was convened at the Thistle Rink of the new Mackay School in 1906. About 4,000 people heard Lieutenant-Governor Bulyea read the Speech from the Throne, followed by a reception in the school.

As might be expected there was some controversy about which city should be the capital of the newly formed province of Alberta. The front runners were Edmonton and Calgary, followed by Red Deer and Banff. Edmonton emerged the winner by a 16 to 8 vote.

Alberta's provincial legislature has 83 members. They are called Members of the Legislative Assembly (MLAs). In 1989, the government was Progressive

Voters used the secret ballot for the first time in the 1878 federal elections.

Conservative and the party standings were PC - 59, NDP - 16, Liberal - 8.

Alberta has 6 senate seats. Appointments to the Senate are made by the prime minister of Canada according to a pre-determined formula of provincial representation. Alberta is entitled to 6 senators. For the first time in Canadian history, Albertans, during the 1989 municipal elections (October 16), also voted for a senate representative (senator). Many Albertans believe we should have an elected senate, and this was a way to try and influence the change. The winner of this history-making senate election was Stan

Waters of the Reform Party of Alberta. The prime minister appointed him to the senate on June 11, 1990.

The lieutenant-governor is the legal head of the provincial executive.

The Honourable W. Helen Hunley, the present lieutenant-governor of Alberta, is the twelfth person, and the first woman, to hold that position.

Andrew Shandro was the first Central European to be elected to a Canadian legislative body. He was elected MLA for the riding of Whitford, Alberta, in 1913, and held that seat until 1921. He was also the youngest member of that body when he was first elected.

Women were given the right to vote in federal elections in 1917.

The first woman cabinet minister in Alberta was The Honourable Irene Parlby (1868 - 1965). She served with the United Farmers of Alberta, as Minister without Portfolio, from 1921 to 1935.

In the early 1930s Major Douglas, a Scottish engineer, formulated the economic theories underlying the Social Credit party ideology. The party thus formed came into power in the Alberta provincial election of 1935 with William Aberhart as its leader.

Government House

The government, under Premier Aberhart, passed the Accurate News and Information Act whereby all published material had to be submitted to the government for approval. The first Pulitzer prize awarded outside the U.S. was given to the *Edmonton Journal* and the weekly *High River Times* for their stand against this act which had originally only been meant to suppress Aberhart's critics. The act was later reworked.

The shortest term of office for any government of Alberta's history was that of the PCs under Premier Don Getty: two years and ten months between 1986 and 1989.

In the federal election of November 21, 1988, the first and only MP to be elected from the New Democratic Party in Alberta was Ross Harvey in the constituency of Edmonton East.

In the federal election of November 21, 1988, the first treaty Indian MP in Canada was elected in the constituency of Wetaskiwin, Alberta. Willie

Littlechild was elected by a vote of 20,057 to his nearest rival at 7,748. He is a member of the Progressive Conservative Party.

The first Reform Party member to be elected member of Parliament was Deborah Grey, in the riding of Beaver River, Alberta, on March 13, 1989. She had almost double the votes of her nearest opponent, Dave Broda, of the PC Party, in the by-election which was called to fill the seat vacated when Tory MP John Dahmer died of cancer five days after winning in the last federal election.

During the 1989 Alberta provincial election, the leaders of the three main parties, PC, ND, and Liberals, all ran in ridings in Edmonton. This occurred once before when Premier E. Manning, CCF Leader Elmer Roper and Liberal Leader J. Harper Prowse all sat as Edmonton MLAs.

In the provincial election of 1989 Premier Getty lost his seat in the riding of Whitemud, in Edmonton, to the

Liberal candidate, Percy Wickman. A by-election was then called in Stettler, at which time (May 9, 1989) Premier Getty won a landslide victory taking 5,559 votes out of a total 7,790.

Mike Cardinal, running for the Progressive Conservative Party during the 1989 Alberta provincial election, became the first Métis to be elected in this province's history.

The only Lord Mayor of London, England born in Canada was Peter Gadsen, who was born in Mannville, Alberta.

Two of Canada's prime ministers were from Alberta: R.B. Bennett, who served from 1930 to 1935, representing Calgary South; and Joe Clark who served from 1979 to 1980, representing Yellowhead.

Roland Michener, former Governor-General of Canada, was born in Lacombe, Alberta.

Alberta was the first province to televise question period at the Legislative Assembly.

Roland Michener monument, with Mount Michener in the background.

THE LEGISLATURE BUILDING OF ALBERTA

Alberta Legislature Building

Alberta's Legislature Building, in Edmonton is the most important building in the province for politics, architecture, and history.

One of the main topics of discussion at the very first session of the Alberta government was that of providing a permanent and suitable building for the government to conduct its business.

Fort Edmonton monument near the Alberta Legislature Building.

The site of the Legislature Building was rapidly agreed upon because of its historical significance and physical prominence. It is on the north bank of the North Saskatchewan River, on the site of the old Hudson's Bay Company fort. Construction began in August of 1907. Although the building had not been completed, the first session of the Legislature began there on November 30, 1911, and the official opening took place on September 3, 1912.

The Provincial Mace

Although you would not know it, the Legislature Building is sitting on quicksand. During construction, concrete pilings reinforced with steel beams were sunk before the footings were laid, so that the building would not shift.

The cornerstone of the Legislature Building was laid on October 1, 1909, by His Excellency The Right Honourable Earl Grey, Governor-General of Canada. The time capsule placed under it contained a set of plans for the building, a list of those who had supervised its construction and a copy of the pay sheet, as well as coins and currency, and copies of the three Edmonton newspapers.

The base of the Legislature Building, including the steps of the east, west, and main entrances, are made of granite quarried on Vancouver Island. Above this is Alberta sandstone from the Glenbow quarry near Calgary. Three types of marble were used inside: green marble from Pennsylvania (base of the chamber); grey marble from Quebec (pillars in the rotunda); and Italian marble (for the railings of the grand staircase and third floor). The main rotunda of the building is open from the well on the first floor to the vaulted dome 53 metres above.

On the floor of the chamber of the legislative assembly is the chair which was originally used by the Speaker of the North-West Territory's first Assembly, which was held in Regina in 1888.

In the centre of the chamber of the legislative assembly is a long table upon which is laid the mace. This table is located directly in front of the Speaker, as the mace is the symbol of the Speaker. It is carried in by the Sergeant-At-Arms at the beginning of each daily sitting and when the speaker leaves, the mace leaves.

Directly south of the Legislature Building near the river is its power plant. It is connected by an underground tunnel to the main building.

PREMIERS OF ALBERTA

Name	Party	Years
Alexander Cameron Rutherford	Liberal	1905-1910
Arthur Lewis Sifton	Liberal	1910-1917
Charles Stewart	Liberal	1917-1921
Herbert Greenfield	United Farmers of Alberta	1921-1925
John Edward Brownlee	United Farmers of Alberta	1925-1934
Richard Gavin Reid	United Farmers of Alberta	1934-1935
William Aberhart	Social Credit	1935-1943
Ernest Charles Manning	Social Credit	1943-1968
Harry Edwin Strom	Social Credit	1968-1971
Peter Lougheed	Conservative	1971-1986
Don Getty	Conservative	1986-

LIEUTENANT GOVERNORS OF ALBERTA

Name	Years
George Hedley Vicars Bulyea	1905-1915
Robert George Brett	1915-1925
William Egbert	1925-1931
William Legh Walsh	1931-1936
Philip Carteret Hill Primrose	1936-1937
John Campbell Bowen	1937-1950
John James Bowlen	1950-1959
John Percy Page	1959-1965
John Walter Grant MacEwan	1965-1974
Ralph G. Steinhauer	1974-1979
Frank C. Lynch-Staunton	1979-1985
Helen Hunley	1985-

LAW AND ORDER

The North-West Mounted Police were established in 1873 and, after a march across the prairies in 1874, they arrived in Alberta and proceeded with their duties of bringing law and order to the west and stopping the illegal whiskey trade. In 1904 they became the Royal North-West Mounted Police and in 1919 they merged with the Dominion Police to form the Royal Canadian Mounted Police.

In 1907 Sheriff Israel Umbach of Stony Plain, Alberta, chained the CNR's locomotive to the tracks to convince the railway to pay its taxes.

Alex Decouteau, in 1909, became the first full-blooded Indian to be hired by a municipal police force in Canada. He rose to the rank of sergeant and also became well known as an athlete when, in 1912, he represented Canada in the Olympic Games held in Sweden. He ran a mile in 4 minutes and 43 seconds, for which King George V gave him one of his gold watches, after the trophy for the event went missing.

The first policewoman to be hired by the City of Edmonton was Annie Jackson in 1912. She was expected to oversee the "morals and manners" of young women.

The Alberta Provincial Police force was formed in 1917 and was responsible for keeping law and order in the province. In 1932 the force was amalgamated with the Royal Canadian Mounted Police (RCMP) by agreement between the provincial and federal governments and thus became part of the main law enforcement agency in Alberta. There are nine municipalities in Alberta which have continued to provide their own police forces. These are Calgary, Camrose, Coaldale, Edmonton, Lacombe, Lethbridge, Medicine Hat, Redcliff and Taber.

Just to the west of Water Valley was the coal mining community of Skunk Hollow. During the prohibition years of the late 1920s, this was also the site of some large stills which produced and supplied Calgary with most of its bootleg whiskey for many years, despite police efforts to find and remove the sources.

In 1987 Alberta had the highest rate of impaired driving charges of all the provinces of Canada - 830 per 100,000 people. Within Alberta, Edmonton had the highest city rate at 814 charges per 100,000 population; this figure was third highest in Canada behind Fredericton, New Brunswick (1,061) and St. John's, Newfoundland (835).

Edmonton's Crime Stoppers program, which began in March of 1983, has cleared almost 3,000 criminal cases to date, recovered $4 million in stolen property, and seized nearly $7.5 million in illicit drugs. Edmonton's program, out of almost 600 in North America, was the most productive for cities with populations of 50,000 to 1,000,000 and this twice earned them the annual Crime Stoppers International Productivity Award. The latest winning was in September of 1989, when they beat out over 700 similar programs around the world, and took top honours at the annual convention held in Albuquerque, New Mexico.

In 1988, Edmonton's City Police became the first police department in Canada to be granted accreditation by the Virginia-based Commission for Accreditation for Law Enforcement Agencies, after it was found they met more than 900 of the commission's policing standards.

Just north of the town of Bowden is the only RCMP dog training facility in Canada. Every major law enforcement agency across Canada has its dogs trained here.

The Code Inquiry, led by Calgary lawyer Bill Code, investigated the failure of Principal Group subsidiaries First Investors Corporation and Associated Investors of Canada. The inquiry began on October 14, 1987, heard 157 witnesses during 205 days and almost six million words of testimony, and ended December 13, 1988. Final arguments of the various interested parties took place from February 6 to 21, 1989. The Code Report was released on July 18, 1989 and the next day charges were laid against Don Cormie (Principal's founder), John Cormie, and executives Ken Marlin and Christa Petracca.

In November of 1988, Thomas Karashowski parachuted off the 95-metre-high Alberta Government Telephone Building in Red Deer. In March 1989 he was fined $150 for the stunt which he admitted in court was " . . . a pretty stupid thing to do."

The motto of the RCMP is "Maintain the Right."

It is the law in Alberta for all passengers and drivers to use seatbelts. This law was struck down as being unconstitutional by a Calgary judge on February 2, 1989, a ruling which caused a lot of controversy. In Edmonton seat belt use was 87%, the highest in Canada. It dropped to about 60% within three weeks of the Calgary ruling. The Crown appealed and seat belts are again mandatory.

MILITARY

During the first world war over 39,000 Albertans served overseas with the Canadian Expeditionary Forces. Of these over 6,000 were killed. Alberta's voluntary response rate for active military service during this period was the highest in Canada.

Located in Jasper National Park is the Victoria Cross Range, a range of mountains which have been named after Alberta winners of the Victoria Cross since World War I. Included are Mount Bazalgette (elevation 2,438 metres), Mount Kerr (elevation 2,560 metres), Mount Kinross (elevation 2,560 metres), Mount Mckean (elevation 2,743 metres), Mount Pattison (elevation 2,316.5 metres), and Mount Zengel (elevation 2,560 metres).

The only Victoria Cross winner actually born in Alberta was Ian Willoughby Bazalgette, born in Calgary on October 19, 1918. He served with the R.A.F. in WWII and died in action on August 4, 1944. His name was installed in Canada's Aviation Hall of Fame in 1973.

During the second world war, 50,844 Albertans joined the army, 19,499 joined the air force, and 7,360 joined the navy. This makes a total enrollment of 77,703; of these, 3,350 lost their lives (1,660 in the army, 1,540 in the air force, and 150 in the navy).

The flags around the main rotunda of the Legislature Building are battalion flags of units from the Edmonton area that served in the two world wars.

During the second world war there was a prisoner-of-war camp at Wainwright. It opened in December 1944. About 1,700 German officers were held here until July 1946. During this period two of them escaped. They were recaptured several weeks later in Texas.

Although Camp Wainwright is not the largest military base in western Canada, it is the main training area for the army. It is one of Canada's best equipped army training grounds and it consists of 624 square kilometres with eighteen weapon ranges and two airfields.

During the Korean War the Canadian Army Special Force, serving with the United Nations Forces in Korea, consisted of 26,791 Canadians, of whom 516 lost their lives.

Sherman Tank at Medicine Hat

This Harvard trainer aircraft is at CFB Penhold.

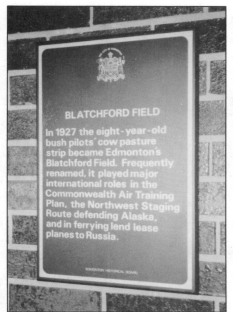

Plaque at Edmonton Municipal Airport

Tank on display in Wallace Park, Wainwright.

T-33 in Leduc

On January 19, 1989, the first woman combat soldier in Canada graduated at Canadian Forces Base Wainwright. Heather Erxleben was one of 16 woman who began the sixteen-week training course (with the men), and she was the only women to complete it. "It is a very physically demanding course," said the 22-year-old Vancouver, B.C. native.

There are only two women fighter jet pilots in active combat squadrons. Both are stationed at CFB Cold Lake, Alberta. Captain Deanna Brasseur and Captain Jane Foster completed a seven-month basic fighter pilot course in January of 1989 on the CF-5 Freedom Fighter.

Thelma Keown of Grande Prairie, Alberta, was one of the first three females to become a part of a Canadian armoured regiment. Along with

Veronica Skinner of Newfoundland, and Mira Fowlie of Winnipeg, the trio joined Lord Strathcona's Horse (Royal Canadian) Regiment based at Calgary.

Military bases are located at, or near, six communities in Alberta: Calgary, Cold Lake, Edmonton, Penhold, Suffield and Wainwright.

The largest military base in Canada is at Suffield, Alberta. It consists of approximately 2,690 square kilometres of land area. With a length of 60 kilometres and a width of 54 kilometres (at the greatest points), it is larger than the combined areas of CFB Gagetown, Valcartier, Petawawa, Shilo and Wainwright. Among its many and varied training areas, CFB Suffield is also a Tactical Air Weapons Range. It is located approximately 50 kilometres northwest of Medicine Hat.

CFB Suffield is also a training area for the British army, called BATUS (British Army Training Unit Suffield).

The training area of CFB Suffield is designated a battle range. CFB Suffield is also a Tactical Air Weapons Range. The range is out of bounds to civilians, as it is dangerous, but it is also considered a wildlife sanctuary.

The only active service prison and detention barracks in the Canadian Forces are located in Edmonton.

The HMCS Nonsuch, Edmonton, got its name from the Hudson's Bay Company ship that sailed into Hudson's Bay in 1668 for the first time.

One of Canada's most famous bush pilots, "Wop" May, was a captain in the Royal Flying Corps in 1918, when he helped bring down the "Red Baron," Manfred von Richthofen. In World War II he supervised the Commonwealth Air Training Plan Schools. (See also transportation chapter.)

T-33 at Edson

At Edson, a T-33 Silver Star jet trainer aircraft is mounted on a pedestal in Centennial Park. It was donated to the Edson Air Cadet Squadron, No. 874, by the Canadian Armed Forces, and was airlifted from Red Deer to Edson. On May 19, 1986, the dedication ceremonies were performed. Centennial Park is located between the east- and west-bound lanes of the Yellowhead Highway.

A CF-104 Star Fighter is located at the junction of Highway 28 and 50th Avenue in Grand Centre. The jet was used in training military personnel and was involved as part of the Canadian contribution to NATO in Europe. It was donated to Grand Centre for its 25th anniversary on April 12, 1983.

CF-104 at Grand Centre

A T-33 jet trainer aircraft, restored by the Royal Canadian Air Cadet Squadron No. 831, of Leduc, was mounted on a pedestal and put on display in front of the Leduc Legion Branch No. 108, at 50th Avenue and 52nd Street on May 7, 1989.

Nanton is known for its Second World War Lancaster Bomber which has been on display since the end of the war.

Lancaster Bomber in Nanton

TRANSPORTATION

RAILWAYS

Railway service in Alberta is provided by the Canadian Pacific Railway (CPR) in the south, Canadian National Railway (CNR) in the central area and the Alberta Resources Railway, Northern Alberta Railway, and the Great Slave Railway in the north.

The building of the transcontinental railway was made possible by people like Father Albert Lacombe who, in 1880, helped negotiate an agreement with the Blackfoot Nation.

The CPR reached Calgary in 1883.

The High Level Bridge at Lethbridge

The last spike on the CPR line going through the North-West Territories (now Alberta) was driven by the wife of superintendent F.P. Brothers. The date was May 27, 1884. A government railway inspector then drove the first spike on the B.C. side, in the Kicking Horse Pass.

The Calgary and Edmonton Railway (C&E) arrived in Strathcona (now south Edmonton) in 1891. A sign at Saskatchewan Drive and 103 Street commemorates this event.

Red Deer was designated as a divisional point on the CNR line between Calgary and Edmonton in 1910.

The oldest railway car in Canada is in the Alberta Pioneer Railway Museum in Namao. It was built in 1877 as a coach car and in 1890 was converted into a baggage car. It was also used in the making of the TV show "The Last Spike."

A private railway which once ran between Rimbey and Lacombe was called the Peanut or Muskeg Special.

The High Level Bridge at Lethbridge is 96 metres high, 1,623 metres long and it spans the Oldman River. It was built in 1909 by the CPR.

The High Level Bridge in Edmonton was completed in 1913 with 8,000 tons of steel held together with 1.4 million rivets. It is nearly 755 metres long and is 53 metres above the North Saskatchewan River. It is used as a roadway and pedestrian crossing, and occasional train crossing. It also used to function as a tramway.

Edmonton's High Level Bridge

The Rochford Railway Bridge

The Rochford Railway Bridge between Mayerthorpe and Sangudo was, at the time it was built, the largest wooden railway trestle bridge in North America.

The East Coulee Trestle Bridge, now closed to vehicular traffic, is the last dual vehicle and railway bridge remaining in western Canada.

The lowest pass in North America traversed by a railway is the Yellowhead Pass. The Grand Trunk Pacific and Canadian Northern railways merged to form the Canadian National Railway, which uses this route.

Two diesel locomotives built in the 1950s were retired after having travelled more than 7 million miles (11,265,100 km) and donated to the city of Medicine Hat in 1985 where they are on display in Riverside Park.

On February 8th, 1986, a train crash near Hinton killed 23 people. The head-on collision, at a combined speed of 173 km/h, between a Via Rail passenger train and a Canadian National freight train, killed 7 railway workers and 16 passengers, and injured 71 others. It took several days before all the bodies could be removed from the wreckage.

On November 21, 1986, 39-year-old Tom Payne of Edmonton gave up his job as an engineer with CPR to go into business for himself. He purchased one of the railway's branch lines, 170 kilometres of track and several engines and other assorted cars and equipment for a total of $2.7 million. With operating expenses of about $2.3 million annually he runs the Central Western Railway, with offices in Edmonton and Stettler. It is the only privately run, short-line railway in Alberta.

On July 1, 1989, another company formed by Mr. Payne, called the Central Western Rail Service Ltd., started running steam tours out of Stettler. Stops are made at points of interest and the service will expand according to demand.

In 1987 railways in Alberta had a total trackage of 10,135.8 kilometres.

HIGHWAYS

Athabasca Landing was founded in 1874 and a trading post was constructed there. Work began on a trail to Edmonton and when this was completed in 1880, it became the first registered highway in Alberta.

The Edmonton-Calgary Stage started its inaugural run on August 6, 1883. It left Jasper House in Edmonton every Monday at 9 a.m. and the trip took 5 days.

The first horseless carriage arrived in Edmonton on May 25, 1904. It was purchased by Mr. J.H. Morris in Winnipeg and was shipped to Edmonton on the train.

H.W. White of Calgary and G.T. Lundy of Innisfail made the first automobile trip from Edmonton to Calgary in March of 1906. The trip took two days.

The road system throughout rural Alberta was laid out by early surveyors. Theoretically, there is a road every mile as you travel east or west, and a road every two miles as you go north or south. The condition of these roads depends on usage and/or population density. Correction lines (roads) run east/west every four townships (38.6 kilometres or 24 miles) and their main purpose is to compensate for the curvature of the earth. The jog, or offsetting, of the north/south roads at correction lines is because of this.

Dunvegan Bridge

Bleriot Ferry

Along some Alberta highways you will see signs designating this to be a CARE highway. CARE stands for Care and Responsibility Every day.

Dunvegan Bridge is Alberta's only suspension bridge for vehicles.

The largest inter-city bus system in Canada, Greyhound Bus Lines Ltd., has its head office in Calgary.

Of the 13 cable ferries that have crossed the Red Deer River, only one remains: the Bleriot Ferry. It was established in 1913.

The longest running ferry operation in Alberta was across the North Saskatchewan River at Victoria Settlement. It shut down in 1972 after running for at least 80 years.

The Rosevear Ferry operating on the McLeod River, connects highways 748 and 16 and operates 24 hours a day from April til October. It is one of the few remaining active ferry operations in Alberta.

Highway 10X, between Rosedale and Wayne, has more bridges than any other comparable piece of road: eleven one-way bridges in nine kilometres.

Our Lady of the Highways shrine, at the east end of Vegreville, is dedicated to the travelling public.

A note of interest in Alberta Report (Nov. - Dec. '89 issue):
"Died: Edna Sutherland, 100, who after travelling to Edmonton from Winnipeg in a Red River cart became the first woman in the city to obtain a driver's license and automobile, in which she was arrested for speeding at 18 miles per hour down Jasper Avenue, and who did volunteer work for the Red Cross in both world wars."

Our Lady of the Highways Shrine, Vegreville

There are five passes through the Rocky Mountains between Alberta and British Columbia. Of these the Yellowhead has the gentlest slopes. The highest point on the Yellowhead Highway is not at the pass (1,120 metres above sea level) but rather at Obed Summit in Alberta (1,164 metres above sea level).

Monkman Pass is a natural pass through the Rocky Mountains from Beaverlodge, Alberta, to Prince George, B.C. It was discovered in the early 1900s by Alex Monkman.

The highest driveable pass in Canada is the Highwood Pass on Highway 40 about 82 kilometres (51 mi.) south of Highway 1 (the Trans-Canada Highway). It is 2,227 metres (7,306 ft.) above sea level.

THE ALASKA HIGHWAY

The highway you are now on leads to the Alaska Highway built by the American army during World War Two from Dawson Creek, British Columbia, to Fairbanks, Alaska. Ten thousand troops and six thousand civilians began construction on March 9, 1942, and completed the 1,523 mile highway in just eight months and thirteen days. It continues to serve as a major transportation link and symbol of friendship and co-operation between Canada and the United States of America.

This sign is on Highway 43, just north of the Yellowhead Highway.

HIGHWAYS & ROADS IN ALBERTA
1987

Paved	18,551 km
Oil Treated	9,350 km
Gravelled	106,043 km
Graded	18,451 km
Total	152,395 km

MOTOR VEHICLE REGISTRATIONS
March 1987

Passenger vehicles	1,306,382
Commercial vehicles	386,035
Trailers	320,438
Motorcycles	42,762
Buses	6,048
Off-highway vehicles	40,496
Other vehicles	12,875
Total	2,115,036

SUMMITS AND PASSES

Crowsnest Pass	elevation 1,396 m
Kicking Horse Pass	elevation 1,647 m
Yellowhead Pass	elevation 1,120 m
Bow Summit (Banff-Jasper Highway)	elevation 2,068 m
Sunwapta Summit (Banff-Jasper Highway)	elevation 2,035 m
Highwood Summit (Bow-Crow Forest Trunk Road)	elevation 2,341 m
Vermilion Pass	elevation 1,640 m

Jasper. Its highest point is at Bow Summit, where it is 2,088 metres (6,850 ft.) above sea level.

Forestry Trunk Road goes some 1,000 kilometres, from Crowsnest Pass north to the Grande Prairie region, and provides access to some of Alberta's forests. This winding gravel road is challenging to drive, but it is beautiful.

Highway 940, a section of the Forestry Trunk Road, is now also known as Big Horn Highway.

The Bow Valley Parkway (Highway 1A) is the alternative road between Banff and Lake Louise through the Bow Valley.

HIGHWAYS MISCELLANEOUS

The Yellowhead Pass and Tête Jaune Cache were named after Pierre Bostonais, an Iroquois man who had light-coloured hair, due to his partially white background. The French voyageurs nicknamed him Tête Jaune, which means "yellowhead."
He came west in the early 1800s and worked for the HBC as a guide and voyageur, and as a hunter and trapper. He was killed by the Beaver Indians in 1827.

Thomas Willey, of England, was Canada's first trans-continental motorist. He left Halifax on August 20, 1921 and arrived in Vancouver in early October. The roads were not great in those days; a couple of times he had to take a train, and he had to take a boat from Sault Ste. Marie to Port Arthur, Ontario. In Alberta, on his way from Calgary to Banff, he was forced to winch his auto over some of the more difficult spots with a block and tackle.

Overall the trip was completed at an average speed of almost 100 miles per day.

Edmonton is the largest city on the Yellowhead Highway and is approximately at the half-way point along the route between Winnipeg, Manitoba and Prince Rupert, B.C. The Yellowhead Highway has a total length of about 3,185 kilometres.

Highway 93, also known as the Icefields Parkway, is considered one of the world's most scenic drives. It runs from Jasper to Lake Louise, passing the Athabasca and Columbia Glaciers and the Sunwapta and Athabasca falls.

The Icefields Parkway was originally a relief project during the depression years of the early 1930s. The highway as we know it today was completed in 1960, and it is 230 kilometres from Highway 1 (near Lake Louise) to

The Akamina Parkway is about 16 kilometres long in the Cameron Valley near Waterton.

In 1754 from a point just north of today's Innisfail, explorer Anthony Henday became the first white man to see the Rocky Mountains. Today the westbound route at this point is known as the Anthony Henday Highway.

The David Thompson Highway starts at Rocky Mountain House and goes 190 kilometres to join the Icefield Parkway.

The Mackenzie Highway is named after the explorer - fur trader who was the first white man to cross the North American continent by land, Alexander Mackenzie. It extends 471 kilometres from Grimshaw to the Northwest Territories border.

Mackenzie Highway sign at Grimshaw

Highway 63 is known as the Fort McMurray Highway.

Highway 33 is known as the Grizzly Trail.

Highway 816 is known as the "Gravel Trail" due to the large gravel pits along this road.

Highway 41 is the Buffalo Trail.

Highways 3, 4, and 61 east from Fort Macleod and Lethbridge are known as the Red Coat Trail.

Sections of Highways 49, 2, and 55 are known as the Northern Woods and Water Route.

Victoria Trail was the original road from Edmonton House to Victoria Settlement. Only parts of this road have been incorporated into today's highway system.

Approximately 10 kilometres east of Highway 21 on Highway 16, there is a cemetery located between the east- and west-bound lanes of traffic.

The Trans-Canada Highway is the longest paved road in the world. It officially opened in 1962 and it measures 7,821 kilometres from Victoria to St. John's, Newfoundland. The Alberta section covers a distance of about 530 kilometres.

The "point of interest" signs you may see along some Alberta roads are really very interesting: that is, if you are able to read them. Some of them are so weather-beaten that it takes study and concentration to get their drifts. (I have been told this will be rectified). However, the signs are very informative and well worth stopping to decipher.

The road signs saying "Buckle up" and "It's the law" were left in place when the mandatory seatbelt law was struck down in February of 1989. The government was successful in its appeal against the decision and seat belts are again mandatory.

HIGHWAYS AND ALCOHOL: SOME SOBERING FACTS

During the past few years the Alberta government has been conducting an extensive program to reduce the devastation and destruction caused by impaired drivers. The following is information from the pamphlets *Alberta Gets Tough On Impaired Driving* and *The Party's Over* from the Alberta Solicitor General's office.

It is estimated that of all fatal collisions in Alberta, up to 40% of them involve the use of alcohol. From 1980 to 1987 there were over 1,250 fatal collisions and 23,000 injury collisions.

Alberta has the highest per capita consumption of alcohol in Canada and there are about 3,400 licensed drinking establishments in the province.

In 1986 there were 19,889 impaired driving charges laid in Alberta. In 1987 this went down slightly to 19,758 and in 1988 there was a very significant drop, down to 18,103. But even this figure represents a ratio of 756 out of every 100,000 people and is the worst in Canada — the national average is 468 for every 100,000.

Alberta is getting tough on impaired drivers; as Solicitor General R.S. (Dick) Fowler says, "Drinking and driving is a serious social issue and commands a comprehensive plan to reduce the incidence of impaired driving. We have 42 impaired driving initiatives which not only focus on enforcement, but also incorporate education and prevention programs."

Monument in Galt Gardens Park, Lethbridge

responded that " . . . your suppositions appear to be correct." This plaque was originally put up at Lethbridge in the early 1960s and ten years later was duplicated for Vancouver. The branch also said " . . . puzzling is the fact that a plaque has stood at Lethbridge for almost two decades, and another for half that time at Vancouver, both containing the same error, and no one has caught it till now . . . the error will, I am sure, be put right in due course."

In 1983 Alberta had three of the ten busiest airports in Canada. Calgary International was fourth (after Toronto, Vancouver and Montreal) with 60,113 flights, 3,533,000 passengers, 8,953,000 kilograms of mail and 29,837,000 kilograms of general cargo. Edmonton International was sixth with 31,401 flights, 1,812,000 passengers, 7,150,000 kilograms of mail and 27,392,000 kilograms of general cargo. Edmonton Municipal was tenth with 12,115 flights, 731,000 passengers, 227,000 kilograms of mail and 1,914,000 kilograms of general cargo.

AIR

An American woman, Katherine Stinson, was the first woman to deliver airmail in Canada. Using a Curtis Biplane in 1918, she carried a bag with 260 pieces of mail from Calgary to Edmonton, landing on the Exhibition Grounds Racetrack. The flight took a little over two hours to complete in good weather.

The first air crossing of the Canadian Rockies was on August 7, 1919. The following is from a plaque in the main terminal building of Vancouver International Airport: "Captain E.C. Hoy made the first crossing of the Canadian Rockies by air. He took off at 4:14 a.m. in his Curtis JN4 (Jenny) and was limited to 7,000 ft. maximum altitude because of his fuel load. He followed a route over Vernon, Grand Forks and Cranbrook. Going through Crawford Pass his Canadian-built plane landed at Lethbridge at 6:22 p.m. He then decided to go on to Calgary [and landed] there at 8:55 p.m." After reading this plaque and thinking about it for some time I came to the conclusion that by Crawford Pass, the writer probably meant Crowsnest Pass. I wrote to the National Historic Parks and Sites Branch in Ottawa and they

The smallest airport in Alberta is located 22 kilometres east and 4 kilometres south of Camrose, on Highway 13. The airport has eight runways for model aircraft manoeuvres. In the hobby shop you'll find sophisticated radio-controlled and remote-controlled jets and planes on display.

There is also a radio-controlled aircraft club in Edmonton. It is known as the Capital City Flyers Club and it has its own field located near the southwest corner of the city.

The site of the first and only UFO landing pad in the world is at St. Paul, Alberta. The platform has provincial and territorial flags displayed and there is also a time-lock container which is to be opened on June 3, 2067 — 100 years after it was built as one of the town's Canada Centennial Projects.

Nanton's WWII Lancaster Bomber, located in Centennial Park is one of six RX-159 bombers left, and was built in 1944.

A summer of aerial entertainment took place in Red Deer in 1988. Major events included the Canadian Sport Parachuting Championships, the Red Deer International Air Show, the World Aerobatic Championships and the Canadian Hot Air Balloon Championships.

Nine-year-old Emma Houlston of Medicine Hat, Alberta, became the youngest person ever to pilot an airplane across Canada when she completed the thirteenth leg of the journey from Sydney, Nova Scotia, to St. John's, Newfoundland, on July 24, 1988. Her father, Paul, a flight instructor, acted as navigator on the 7775-kilometre trip which began July 10th at Victoria, B.C. The entire trip was videotaped as proof for the Guinness Book of World Records.

Mark Bushrod and instructor Reg Blackwell. Mark is making his first flight.

Joanna Mullen, of Edmonton, became the youngest pilot in Canada on March 13, 1989 when she received her license on her seventeenth birthday.

Canada's Aviation Hall of Fame is located in Edmonton, Alberta. It focuses on the personalities, past and present, of persons who have contributed to Canadian aviation. The hall occupies 1800 square metres of first-class exhibition space, has an excellent reference library, and was founded in 1973. As of June 2, 1989 the hall had 133 inductees: 131 men and two women. It is located in the Edmonton Convention Centre on Jasper Avenue.

The book *Edmonton . . . The Way it Was*, has this to say about early flying in Alberta: "Both Edmonton and the north owe much to the legendary bush pilots Punch Dickins, "Wop" May, Grant McConnachie and Matt Berry. The four former war aces helped to open up the north, supplying vital lifelines to remote communities."

St. Paul's UFO Landing Pad

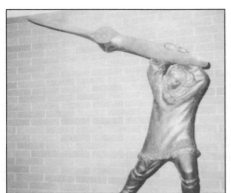

Statue at Canada's Aviation Hall of Fame

May Lake, in the northwestern corner of Alberta, is named after Wilfred Reid "Wop" May, (1896-1952), one of Alberta's and Canada's outstanding pioneers of flying in the north country. His many accomplishments in this field resulted in his being admitted to Canada's Aviation Hall of Fame. (See also military chapter.)

A plaque commemorating the achievements of Wop May, put up by the Historic Sites and Monuments Board of Canada, is located on the ground floor of the main terminal building at Edmonton's Municipal Airport.

McConachie Lake, located in the area between Slave Lake and Fort McMurray, was named after George William Grant McConachie, another one of Alberta's and Canada's outstanding bush pilots in the 1930s and '40s. He was instrumental in setting up the Canadian Pacific Airlines and turning it into an international carrier. Mr. McConachie was named to Canada's Aviation Hall of Fame in 1973.

McMullen Lake, north of Slave Lake, was named after Archie McMullen, a well known Alberta bush pilot of the 1930s. He was a test pilot during the second world war and was named to Canada's Aviation Hall of Fame in 1973.

SPORTS

Every year over 100,000 athletes, coaches, officials and volunteers are involved in the Alberta Summer and Winter Games. Participants qualify through zone games. The summer games are held on odd-numbered years and the winter games are in even-numbered years.

The 1989 Summer Games were held in Brooks, and for the first time a triathlon event was included. (A triathlon is a three-event race consisting of swimming, running, and cycling.)

The Alberta Seniors Games are supported by the Alberta Sports Council. The games are held every even-numbered year and are open to everyone over the age of fifty-five.

The Eleventh Commonwealth Games, considered to be the second most important amateur athletic event in the world, were held in Edmonton August 3 - 12, 1978. It was the third time these games have been held in Canada. (The first time was at Hamilton in 1930 and the second time was in Vancouver in 1954 — note the 24-year intervals). Competing in these games were athletes from 48 countries. Edmonton's Commonwealth Stadium, built for this event, has a seating capacity of 60,217 and is home to the Edmonton Eskimos football team. These games were opened by Queen Elizabeth II.

Edmonton was the site of the World University Games in 1983.

Edson is the home of western Canada's largest Mixed Slo-Pitch Tournament.

Mannville hosts the Mammoth Softball Tournament in mid-July. This annual event is the largest tournament of its kind in western Canada.

Olds was host to the 1986 World Plowing Match.

The Jasper-Banff Relay Race is held in early June of each year and runners from around the world race from Jasper to Banff.

The Alberta Sports Hall of Fame and Museum consists of memorabilia and photographs on Alberta's sports heritage. Included are uniforms and equipment from the 1982 Mount Everest Expedition and past World Cup ski races and a curling display. It is located in the Petro-Canada Centre in Calgary.

There are over 200 golf courses in Alberta.

The Kananaskis Country Golf Course is the only 36-hole golf course in Alberta. It has 4 nine-hole loops which start and end at the clubhouse, making it possible to play a number of combinations.

Roy Blowes of Calgary originally took up playing darts as a form of physical therapy for his rheumatoid arthritis in 1982. Now, the 1989 Guinness Book of World Records lists him as being the only person to ever score 501 points with just nine darts.

The Edmonton Grads was a women's basketball club started by Dr. J. Percy Page in 1915. From 1915 to 1922 the team played and won 147 games. From 1922, when permanent records commenced, until 1940, they played 375 games and only lost 20. Their list of trophies and titles included everything right up to World Champions. In 1989 a new park in Edmonton's Westmount area was named after this team. An Edmonton high school is also named after Percy Page. Page went on to become Alberta's lieutenant governor (1959-1965).

Back in the 1920s Edmonton established a world record for per capita betting at the horse races. This record has held, with some slight variations, right up to the present time.

On August 6, 1988, the English Channel was swum for the first time by an Albertan, John Cormier, a firefighter from Red Deer. His swim took 11 hours and 44 minutes and was carried out in an effort to raise funds for the pediatric unit of the Red Deer Regional Hospital.

The World Junior Curling Championships were held in Medicine Hat from March 13 to 19, 1983.

The Ryan Express curling team, headed by skip Pat Ryan, became the first team in almost twenty years to win the national title of the Labatt Brier two years in a row. Other team members were: third - Randy Ferbey, second - Don Walchuk, and lead - Don McKenzie. Their win came on March 12, 1989, after a dismal start, and they went on to win the World Championships which were held at Milwaukee, Wisconsin, on April 2 to 9, 1989.

The LaDawn Funk curling team, from Spruce Grove, Alberta, won the World Junior Ladies Championships at Markham, Ontario, on March 26, 1989. This was the second year of this event and Canada won it the first year as well, when Julie Sutton's team from B.C. came out on top. Along with skip LaDawn Funk were teammates Laurelle Funk (LaDawn's sister) - lead, Cindy Larsen - second, and Sandy Symyrozum - third.

Kurt Browning of Caroline, Alberta, won the gold medal in men's figure skating at the world championships in Paris on March 16, 1989. Included in his performance were six triple jumps including a triple-triple combination. He won the gold again in 1990, when the championships were held in Halifax, Nova Scotia.

Radya Cherkaoui, 15, of Edmonton, became the first Canadian woman to win an international competition in Tae Kwon Do. She won the gold medal in the women's lightweight division at the Junior Tae Kwon Do Championships held at Colorado Springs in August of 1989. Ariel Del Rosario of Edmonton won a bronze medal in the boys featherweight division, Kerri Drummond of St. Albert won a bronze medal in the women's featherweight division, and Tara Gosselin of Whitecourt won a bronze medal in the women's bantamweight division.

Besides teams in the CFL and NHL, Alberta has at least four other professional sports teams. These are the Edmonton Trappers and the Calgary Cannons of the Pacific Coast Baseball League, and the Edmonton Brickmen and the Calgary Strikers of the Canadian Soccer League.

The Northlands Coliseum in Edmonton opened on November 10, 1974.

The Olympic Saddledome in Calgary opened on October 15, 1983.

HOCKEY

The Allan Cup is the top prize of amateur hockey in Canada. The first team to bring the Allan Cup to Alberta was the Calgary Stampeders in 1945/46. The Edmonton Flyers won it in 1947/48, and the Drumheller Miners won it in 1965/66. Other notable hockey teams from Alberta were the Lacombe Rockets (world tour in 1964), the Camrose Maroons (Alberta champs 1978/79), the Innisfail Eagles (Alberta senior "A" champs 1981/82) and the Edmonton Mercurys (Intermediate Hockey World Champs in 1950).

Medicine Hat is the home of the Canadian Junior Hockey Champions, the Medicine Hat Tigers. They were the 1987-1988 Memorial Cup Winners.

There are only two provinces in Canada that have more than one team playing in the NHL: Alberta & Quebec.

Northlands Coliseum, Edmonton

ALBERTA TEAMS IN STANLEY CUP PLAYOFF FINALS

Date	Winning Team	Losing Team	Games Played
1922/23	Ottawa	Vancouver/Edmonton	3/2
1923/24	Montreal	Vancouver/Calgary	2/2
1982/83	N.Y. Islanders	Edmonton	4
1983/84	Edmonton	N.Y. Rangers	5
1984/85	Edmonton	Philadelphia	5
1985/86	Montreal	Calgary	5
1986/87	Edmonton	Philadelphia	7
1987/88	Edmonton	Boston	4
1988/89	Calgary	Montreal	6
1989/90	Edmonton	Boston	5

Notes:
- In the 1922/23 series noted above Ottawa played two games against Vancouver and one against Edmonton, winning two for the cup.
- In the 1923/24 series Montreal defeated Vancouver and then Calgary with one game in each city, to win the Stanley Cup.
- The Edmonton team in 1922/23 was the Edmonton Eskimos and the Calgary team was the Calgary Tigers.

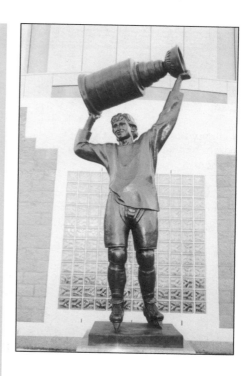

The National Hockey League merged with the World Hockey Association (WHA) in the 1979/80 season.

The 40th NHL All-Star Game was held in Edmonton on February 7, 1989. The Campbell Conference beat the Wales Conference 9-5. The return of Wayne Gretzky of the Los Angeles Kings to play in Edmonton was cause for considerable excitement and the fans were not let down.

Val Fonteyne, of Wetaskiwin, Alberta, has an NHL hockey record that will probably never be matched. He played hockey in the WHA for two years and the NHL for 13 years, from 1957 to 1972, for a total of 969 games in 15 years. His record: a total of 30 minutes in penalty time. This has earned him the nickname Mr. Clean.

The Edmonton Oilers have been in six Stanley Cup series finals, winning five of them. The first one was in 1984.

Wayne Gretzky holds, or shares in, at least 42 NHL records, most of which were acquired while he was with the Edmonton Oilers.

Wayne Gretzky broke Gordie Howe's all-time points record of 1850 points by scoring a goal just 53 seconds before the end of the third period in a game between the Los Angeles Kings and the Edmonton Oilers on October 15, 1989. The game was at Edmonton and the Kings, the team for which Gretzky was playing, won by a score of 5 to 4 in overtime.

Wayne Gretzky's first two professional goals were scored against the Edmonton Oilers.

On March 12, 1989, Wayne Gretzky scored his first goal against the Edmonton Oilers since he played for the World Hockey Association Indianapolis Racers.

The Edmonton Oilers joined the World Hockey Association (WHA) in 1972. The Oilers were originally called the Alberta Oilers.

The Calgary Cowboys were the predecessors of the Calgary Flames. They were disbanded in 1978 and, two years later, on May 21, 1980, the Atlanta Flames officially became the Calgary Flames.

Calgary has been in two Stanley Cup Series and they won one of them; on May 25, 1989, they beat the Montreal Canadiens 4-2 in the sixth game, which was held in Montreal.

FOOTBALL

Edmonton has been in 18 Grey Cup games and emerged the winner in 11 of them.

Calgary has been in five Grey Cup games and emerged the winner in two of them.

The only Grey Cup game played in Edmonton was on November 18, 1984, when Winnipeg defeated Hamilton 47-17.

The only Grey Cup Game played in Calgary was on November 23, 1975, when Edmonton defeated Montreal 9-8.

One of the coldest Grey Cup games ever played was at Calgary in 1975. It was -11°C and with the wind chill factor it was the equivalent of -22°C. The Canadian Weather Trivia Calendar notes "This particular contest was memorable for two things. One was the total absence of touchdowns. The other was a pre-game incident in which a shoeless, topless, young woman cavorted before the 33,000 spectators to become the world's coldest streaker."

ALBERTA TEAMS IN GREY CUP GAMES

YEAR	WINNER	LOSER	SCORE
1921	Toronto	Edmonton	23-0
1922	Queen's University	Edmonton	13-1
1948	Calgary	Ottawa	12-7
1949	Montreal	Calgary	28-15
1952	Toronto	Edmonton	21-11
1954	Edmonton	Montreal	26-25
1955	Edmonton	Montreal	34-19
1956	Edmonton	Montreal	50-27
1960	Ottawa	Edmonton	16-6
1968	Ottawa	Calgary	24-21
1970	Montreal	Calgary	23-10
1971	Calgary	Toronto	14-11
1973	Ottawa	Edmonton	22-18
1974	Montreal	Edmonton	20-7
1975	Edmonton	Montreal	9-8
1977	Montreal	Edmonton	41-6
1978	Edmonton	Montreal	20-13
1979	Edmonton	Montreal	17-9
1980	Edmonton	Hamilton	48-10
1981	Edmonton	Ottawa	26-23
1982	Edmonton	Toronto	32-16
1986	Hamilton	Edmonton	39-15
1987	Edmonton	Toronto	38-36

Note - The Edmonton team of 1921 were called the Edmonton Elks.

SKIING

The sport of skiing was introduced in Alberta by early Norwegian settlers in the 1890s and there are now more than forty ski areas in the province.

Lake Louise is Canada's largest individual ski area and year-round resort. The average skier can ski any one of three separate and distinct mountain faces and would have to stay a week to ski every run. The Lake Louise ski area is rated 30% expert, 45% intermediate and 25% novice. The highest elevation in the area is 2,636 metres and the total vertical rise is 991 metres.

The first World Cup Downhill Ski Event ever held in Canada was in 1980 at Lake Louise. The Lake Louise course is one of the top three downhill courses in the world.

The first ski lift installed at Lake Louise was in 1954.

The most extensive non-mountain ski area in Alberta is the Canyon Ski Area in Red Deer. It has 11 runs with lights for night skiing.

The highest ski resort in the Canadian Rockies is Sunshine Village just outside (above) Banff. To get there, one takes the longest gondola ride in Canada, which is five kilometres long.

Sunshine Village gets more natural snow per year and has a longer season than any other resort in Alberta.

Sunshine Village has 61 named runs served by a quad chair, a triple chair, four double chairs, three T-bars, two beginner tows, and the gondola. The Sunshine ski area is rated 20% expert, 60% intermediate, and 20% novice. The Angel Express quad chair moves 2,400 skiers per hour. The area's highest elevation is 2,730 metres. It has a vertical rise of 1,070 metres, and the longest run is about 8 kilometres. Total lift capacity is 15,200 per hour.

Marmot Basin, located in Jasper National Park, has one triple chair, three double chairs, and three T-bars. The total lift capacity is 8,684 skiers per hour. The area has a total vertical rise of 701 metres with its highest elevation at 2,423 metres.

Based on the population of those aged 12 and over, the Canadian Ski Council reports one out of every four Canadians is active in the sport of skiing. Cross country and alpine skiing are two of the five most popular winter sports in Canada. In Alberta there are about 604,000 downhill skiers and 439,000 cross country skiers.

RODEOS

Guy Weadick, considered to be the founder of the Calgary Stampede in 1912, was chosen in 1976 to be a member of the Rodeo Hall of Fame in Oklahoma City, Oklahoma.

Since its inception in 1912, the Calgary Stampede has become known as the Greatest Outdoor Show On Earth.

One of the world's most dangerous sports is chuckwagon racing. This is one of the main features of the Calgary Stampede, where it originated in 1923, and is today a highly competitive and "big money" event.

The oldest annual rodeo in Alberta is held in July each year at Dogpound. In the old days this was a popular Cree Indian camp and hunting area.

Teepee Creek, east of Sexsmith or northeast of Grande Prairie, is the site of Canada's largest amateur stampede.

OLYMPICS

The Olympic motto is *citius, altius, fortius,* which is Latin meaning "faster, higher, braver." The Olympic symbol is five interlocking rings representing sporting friendship of all people of all the five continents: Africa, America (North and South), Asia, Australia, and Europe. The rings are black, blue, green, red and yellow, on a white background. At least one of these colors is in the national flag of every country. The olympic flame symbolizes the continuity between the ancient and modern olympic games.

The Canadian olympic team for the 1988 Summer Olympics at Seoul, South Korea, consisted of 350 athletes, 43 of which were from Alberta. The administration office for Canada's olympic team is in the Saddledome stadium in Calgary.

The Olympic Saddledome in Calgary has the world's largest free-span concrete roof. The building seats 17,000 people and hosts over 115 events each year. It was opened in 1983.

Mount Nakiska sign and viewpoint on Highway 40

Olympic Park, Calgary

1988 WINTER OLYMPIC GAMES

November 17, 1987 - The olympic torch began its 87-day, 18,000-kilometre journey from St. John's, Newfoundland, to Calgary, Alberta. Some 6,820 Canadians carried the torch on its way beginning with former olympians Barbara Ann Scott and Fred Hayward.

On February 13, 1988, the last person to carry the 1988 Winter Olympics Torch, and the one to light the olympic cauldron, was 11-year-old Albertan Robyn Perry. On February 12, 1989, she rekindled the olympic flame to open Calgary's Winter Festival.

When the 1988 Winter Olympic Games at Calgary were over, the following was reported in the 1989 Canadian Weather Trivia Calendar: "The Winter Olympics opened at Calgary under partially cloudy skies, with a temperature of -4.9°C and winds gusting to 74 km/h. Above normal winds and temperatures were the main weather story of the games."

It is estimated that 2.5 billion people watched the opening ceremonies of the 1988 Calgary Winter Olympics on television. These were the first winter olympics to be hosted by Canada and they were the largest ever, with about 1,759 athletes from 57 participating countries.

At the 1988 Calgary Winter Olympics, Canada won five medals. Skier Karen Percy, of Banff, was Canada's only multiple medal winner and she was also the only non-European to win any of the 30 medals in the alpine skiing events. Canada's athletes were impressive in the categories of personal bests and top eight performances, and they also captured 14 firsts in demonstration sports. (Demonstration sports are those being considered as possible future olympic events).

During the XV Winter Olympic Games at Calgary, the Calgary Tower became the tallest olympic torch in history at 190.8 metres.

Olympic Park at Calgary is Canada's newest world-class sporting facility. It includes the Olympic Hall of Fame, the world's largest olympic museum, with three full floors of exhibits featuring Canada's involvement in the olympic movement.

ARTS AND ENTERTAINMENT

Albertans are the largest consumers of cultural products in Canada.

The oldest professional arts institute in Alberta is the Edmonton Art Gallery which was incorporated as the Edmonton Museum of Art in 1924.

Dinosaur Valley, near Drumheller, is known as the most paintable valley in Canada's West.

The Northern Alberta Jubilee Auditorium in Edmonton was built in 1955 to celebrate Alberta's 50th birthday. It has 2,700 seats and is home to arts groups including the Edmonton Symphony Orchestra, the Alberta Ballet, the Edmonton Opera and various theatre companies.

The Southern Alberta Jubilee Auditorium, in Calgary, was opened in 1955 simultaneously with its twin in Edmonton. It has 2,719 seats in the auditorium, as well as a 250-seat Dr. Betty Mitchell Theatre, and meeting and banquet rooms.

Edmonton is the theatre capital of western Canada, the home of 14 professional theatre companies. Edmonton has more live theatre per capita than any other city in North America.

The biggest festival in Canada is the Edmonton Folk Music Festival held in Gallagher Park for three days during the first week in August. The tenth annual festival was held in 1989.

The Canadian Country Music Hall of Honour is located in the Edmonton Convention Centre. It was dedicated in 1987 and consists of plaques honoring outstanding Canadian country music entertainers. To date, there are plaques in the hall honoring the following nine inductees: Papa Joe Brown, Wilf Carter, John Richard (Jack) Feeney, Tommy Hunter, Don Messer, William Harold Moon, Orval Prophet, Hank Snow and Lucille Starr. Plans are now underway to build Canada's first museum to honor Canada's country music artists.

Ian Tyson, one of the top country music artists in North America, is an Albertan. He operates his own ranch at Longview.

"Flying Fingers" Al Cherny, one of Canada's greatest violinists (fiddler), passed away in August 1989 at the age of 56. He was born in Medicine Hat, Alberta, and had been a regular on the Tommy Hunter Show for almost 25 years. He will be very sadly missed by many.

During the 1989 Juno Awards, held in Toronto March 12, k.d. lang, of Consort, Alberta, won the two highest awards for female artists in Canada. These were Best Female Vocalist and Best Country Female Vocalist.

At the World Highland Dance competition, which was held in Scotland in early September 1989, Estelle Clewes of Sherwood Park, Alberta, won the title in the 13-year-old age bracket.

The Red Barn at the Alberta Wildlife Park has the largest indoor barbecue facilities in Canada, providing 2500 square metres for dining and dancing. Friday and Saturday nights are dedicated to Old Time Dancing, and Wednesday is bingo night.

The Red Barn

The second tallest pavilion at Expo '86 in Vancouver was the very popular Alberta Pavilion. It was 32.45 metres in height.

The Whitemud Drive Amusement Park, in Edmonton, has the only bumper boat pond in Alberta. The boats are equipped with Honda engines and may be used by eight year olds and up. There are also children's bumper boats for four- to eight-year-olds.

The largest Blackjack tournament north of Nevada is held in Edmonton during Klondike Days. It began in 1985 and is sponsored by No. 7 cigarettes and radio station CFRN.

Premier A.C. Rutherford, in 1907, put forth a bill in the legislature to establish public libraries.

The Edmonton Public Library has the highest circulation figures in the country. Almost every community in the province has access to a library; there are more than 300 public libraries in Alberta.

The reference section of the Edmonton Public Library recently purchased the new second edition of the Oxford English Dictionary. It has over 500,000 words in 20 volumes (total 22,000 pages) and weighs 64.4 kilograms (142 lb.). The price: $3,125.00 per set.

The town of Falher claims to have the largest volume of French-language materials of any municipal library west of Quebec.

Alberta has over 30 publishers and has the second largest publishing industry in English Canada. Alberta also has the second largest indigenous film and video industry in English Canada.

The Writers Guild of Alberta has about 800 members, many of them contributors to periodicals, journals and newspapers throughout the world.

Edmonton's Klondike Days, held for ten days in July every year, is a time when residents dress up in "gay nineties" apparel and celebrate a past era when Edmonton was the start-off point for the overland contingents of the Klondike Gold Rush. It is Canada's biggest and greatest costume party.

The wicket clerks at Postal Station E in Edmonton dressed up for Klondike Days.

Edmonton's Heritage Festival, held every August at Hawrelak Park, portrays the ethnic diversity of Alberta's people. It includes displays, entertainment and foods from different ethnic communities and countries. Based on the recommendations of the Alberta Cultural Heritage Council, Heritage Day was established in Alberta in 1974. The Alberta Heritage Day Act states "The first Monday in August in each year shall be kept and observed as a day of public celebration and known as Alberta Heritage Day." The first Heritage Day was held on August 5, 1974, and was celebrated in Edmonton and Calgary. In 1988, Heritage Day celebrations were held in 33 Alberta communities.

TOURIST ATTRACTIONS

For information on tourist zones call Travel Alberta toll free at 1-800-222-6501 from within Alberta, 427-4321 in the Edmonton area, or 1-800-661-8888 from outside the province.

There are over 1,000 campgrounds in Alberta.

Alberta Fish and Wildlife stocks some 330 lakes with about six million fish per year.

The grave, statue and commemorative sign for Twelve Foot Davis are on the northwest side of a hill near Peace River overlooking the confluence of the Smoky and Peace rivers. Henry Fuller Davis was a prospector in the Cariboo gold fields of British Columbia and he once filed a twelve-foot claim between two larger ones and made a small fortune out of it. He

settled in the Peace River area and was known as a big-hearted man who never locked his door.

Miette Hot Springs, east of Jasper, are the warmest hot springs in the Canadian Rockies. Water is collected from three springs and mixed with cold water before pouring into the pools, where the average temperature is 39°C.

The Great Divide Waterfall is a man-made waterfall that cascades from Edmonton's High Level Bridge on Canada Day and other special occasions. The 8,000-ton steel bridge, which came into use in 1913, was used as the superstructure for the man-made waterfall, which was turned on for the first time in 1980 to commemorate Alberta's 75th Anniversary.

Twelve Foot Davis

Sylvan Lake has been a popular summer resort area since 1901.

Calaway Park, located 9.6 kilometres west of Calgary on Highway 1, claims to be Canada's largest theme park. The 24-hectare park is open during the summer season.

The Columbia Icefield is one of the greatest accumulations of ice south of the Arctic. It is one of the most fascinating and accessible icefields in North America. About an hour's drive south of Jasper on the Icefields Parkway (Highway 93), it lies astride the B.C.-Alberta boundary and it covers an area of about 389 square kilometres to depths of 600 - 900 metres, and 130 square kilometres of it are at, or higher than, 2550 metres above sea level.
The *Canadian Encyclopedia* describes the Columbia Icefield as being " . . . at

the geographic and hydrographic apex of North America, at the point from which all land falls away."

The boundary between Jasper and Banff national parks occurs at Sunwapta Pass, 108 kilometres south of Jasper. It is from this pass that the headwaters of the North Saskatchewan and Sunwapta rivers flow in opposite directions. The North Saskatchewan flows to Hudson's Bay and the Sunwapta flows to the Arctic via the Athabasca and Mackenzie rivers.

At the top of Sulphur Mountain, high above Banff, is the Panoramic Summit Restaurant — the highest restaurant in Canada.

At the Sam Livingstone Fish Hatchery and Rearing Station, at Calgary, Alberta, five to seven million fish are produced annually to stock Alberta's rivers, streams and lakes.

The Mount Lorette Fishing Ponds, which can be found 17 kilometres from Highway 1 on Highway 40, have been designed specifically to accommodate wheelchair fishermen.

The name "badlands" was derived from a translation of the words *mauvaises terres* which early French traders used to describe the rugged terrain of that section of the Red Deer River Valley which is one of Alberta's most fascinating places. This semi-desert area of Alberta is a very popular tourist attraction.

Medicine Hat, Alberta, claims to have the longest and most exciting water slides in western Canada. The Riverside Waterslide has twelve slides totalling over 800 metres in length. Also at the site is a 150-person capacity whirlpool, the largest in Canada.

Punch Bowl Falls near Pocahontas on the Miette Hot Springs road.

WEST EDMONTON MALL

The West Edmonton Mall (WEM) is described as "the world's largest fun, fashion and entertainment centre." It has been listed in the Guinness Book of World Records. This "eighth wonder of the world" covers approximately 24 square city blocks of ground space and includes the following:
 - 210 fashion shops for women
 - 35 menswear stores
 - 55 shoe stores
 - 35 jewellery stores
 - 19 movie theatres
 - 110 eating establishments
 - a par-46, 18-hole mini golf course

There are large department stores and many other stores and services totalling over 800. The Fantasyland Hotel features theme rooms such as the Truck, Polynesian, Arabian, Roman and Victorian Coach rooms.
The mall is home to the world's largest indoor amusement park including the world's largest indoor triple-loop roller coaster and the thirteen-storey Drop of Doom. Here, the world's largest

waterpark can be found, which can accommodate 5,000 people and has a temperature of 30°C (86°F). The wave pool is promoted as the world's largest, containing about 12.3 million litres of water and equipped with a 1,200 hp motor to make 1.5-metre waves. Of the 23 waterslides, The Twister is promoted as the longest slide in the world, at 225 metres.

The full-size replica of Christopher Columbus' flagship, the Santa Maria, in West Edmonton Mall

A full-size replica of Christopher Columbus's flagship, the *Santa Maria*, is in the same pool as the submarine rides. On the submarines you may view dolphins, sharks, and other exotic fish. Dolphin shows are held several times daily. The Edmonton Oilers occasionally practice at the NHL-sized skating rink, which is open to the public. Outside the mall there is parking space for 30,000 vehicles (20,000 cars around the mall, plus an additional parking lot which holds 10,000 cars and RVs). One wing of the mall is a re-creation of Bourbon Street in New Orleans, home to 13 nightclubs. The mall also has the world's first indoor rickshaws.

The submarines

Aerial view of West Edmonton Mall

Some of the fountains at the mall

Around the corridors of West Edmonton Mall are many fountains and pools. People quite often throw coins into these pools, which are gathered up on a regular basis and donated to charities to benefit the young, the elderly and the handicapped.

World Waterpark at West Edmonton Mall

The NHL-sized skating rink

SMILE

You're A Tourist Attraction

ZOOS

Polar Park, formerly known as the Alberta Game Farm, is located just east of Sherwood Park, at Edmonton's southeast corner. It is owned and operated by Dr. Al Oeming, world-renowned zoologist. The park consists of over 1,000 rare, exotic and, in some cases, endangered species. The park's mandate is the preservation and breeding of animal species indigenous to cold climates. It is open year-round.

The Alberta Wildlife Park, near Legal, Alberta, is home to Canada's largest collection of African hoofed animals. The park contains some 2,500 animals and birds from all over the world — all in a scenic 400-hectare natural setting.

St. George's Island Zoo in Calgary is Canada's second largest zoo. It contains over 1,400 animals plus a tropical aviary-conservatory with over 11,000 plants. Also included is the world-class Prehistoric Park with life-size displays of dinosaurs in their natural habitats.

Reptile World, formerly of Strathmore, now in Drumheller, has Canada's largest public reptile display.

Snakes, lizards, frogs and toads, turtles and many others are included in over 60 displays, totalling about 250 animals in all.

The Brooks Wildlife Centre is the only government facility in Alberta to produce ring-necked pheasant. From their own breeding stock, over 10,000 eggs are hatched each year and, when it is safe to do so, the chicks are released to their natural habitat in the wild.

On the north end of Main Street, in Oyen, Alberta, is a statue of a pronghorn, an animal common in this area. The pronghorn's eyes are as big as a horse's and he can see small objects several kilometres away.

MUSEUMS

At least 75 communities in Alberta have museums.

The Provincial Museum, located in Edmonton, has 3600 square metres of permanent exhibit space in four major galleries, and covers millions of years of Alberta's history in the areas of earth sciences, animals, man and nature.

The Glenbow Centre and Museum opened in September 1976 in Calgary. The museum was inspired by Eric Harvie, a man who struck it rich when oil was discovered on his grazing lands, who also collected pioneer artifacts. In 1966 he presented his entire collection, and a large endowment fund, to the people of Alberta. The Glenbow Museum complex has, among other things, the largest collection of Canadiana in the world.

Historic Fort Edmonton is laid out to represent three distinct eras in Edmonton's history. The three streets within the fort are named 1885 Street, 1905 Street and 1920 Street, and each one is a re-creation of Edmonton in that time period.

Entrance to Fort Edmonton

Joseph B. Tyrrell discovered dinosaur bones in the Red Deer River Valley while doing a coal survey for the Geological Survey of Canada in 1884. The Tyrrell Museum of Palaeontology is located a short distance from where Tyrrell made the first significant

Display near entrance to Calgary Zoo

Tyrrell Museum of Palaeontology

Edmonton's Space Sciences Centre

discovery of dinosaur remains in Alberta. His find was named Alberto-saurus and has since been followed by the discovery of the fossilized remains of some 35 species of dinosaurs in Dinosaur Provincial Park. The museum is set on an eight-hectare site occupying 29,120 square kilometres including 11440 square kilometres of display area, a 200-seat auditorium, a 375-seat cafeteria, a library, a laboratory and research offices. It was officially opened on September 25, 1985, and about 500,000 people visit it per year.

One of the finest private fossil collections in Alberta is located in the Drumheller Dinosaur and Fossil Museum.

The Reynolds Museum at Wetaskiwin contains one of North America's largest collections of antique cars, tractors, steam engines, fire engines and airplanes.

The Sir Alexander Galt Museum in Lethbridge covers the city's history through its beginning as a coal-mining town to its present stature as "the irrigation capital of Canada."

The Clerk's Quarters of the 1864 Hudson's Bay Company post at Victoria Settlement is the oldest building in Alberta still on its original site.

The Remington-Alberta Carriage Collection Interpretive Centre and Alberta Museum of Horse-drawn Vehicles will be opened in Cardston in 1991. The collection was started in the 1950s by Don Remington and has since developed into the largest of its kind in Canada and the second largest in North America.

The oldest natural history museum in western Canada is the Banff Park Museum. It features the wildlife and natural history of the parks of western Canada.

Edmonton's Space Sciences Centre includes Canada's largest, most advanced and most dynamic planetarium. The centre has a star theatre, western Canada's first IMAX Theatre and an exhibit gallery. The Margaret Zeidler Star Theatre is the largest theatre of its kind in Canada: about 23 metres across and 14 metres high. The Devonian Theatre shows IMAX film, a special type of system that makes the images seem three-dimensional.

The Bruderheim Meteorite, a 4.6 billion-year-old rock, is one of the many interesting displays at the centre. Also on display is a piece of moon rock which was picked by astronaut Dave Scott of the Apollo 15 mission in 1971. Other fascinating items and displays include hands-on science demonstration games for the kids.

The Donalda Lamp Museum has over 650 lamps and other assorted and related items.

Reynolds Museum, Wetaskiwin

NATURAL FEATURES

LAND

In Canada, Alberta is fourth in size in land area, forest area, and population.

Area	661,185 km²
Land	644,389 km²
Water	16,796 km²

The southern half of Alberta's western border has never been measured. It follows the Rocky Mountains' "height of land" (mountain peaks and ridges) which would be almost impossible to measure. The lengths of the rest of Alberta's borders are known. The east border, shared with Saskatchewan, is 1,170 kilometres long. The north border, shared with the Northwest Territories, is 580 kilometres long. To the south, the border shared with Montana is 295 kilometres in length.

Alberta at its widest point (55°) is 660 kilometres across, and at its longest point (114°) it is 1,208 kilometres.

Montana is the only state that borders on Alberta.

There are six ports of entry between Alberta and Montana. These are at Aden, Alta./Whitlash, Mont.; Carway, Alta./Piegan, Mont.; Chief Mountain, Alta.; Coutts, Alta./Sweetgrass, Mont.; Del Bonita, Alta.; and Wildhorse, Alta.

The highest point in Alberta is Mount Columbia at an altitude of 3747 metres. It straddles the B.C./Alta. border off the Banff-Jasper (Icefields) Highway. (The highest point in the Canadian Rockies is Mount Robson at 3954 metres above sea level. It also straddles the B.C./Alta. border but it peaks on the B.C. side.)

Mount Columbia

The lowest point in Alberta is on the Slave River at the Northwest Territories border, 175 metres above sea level.

The Cypress Hills of southeast Alberta are somewhat of an oddity. They rise suddenly to a 1462-metre-high plateau from the prairie below, and are the highest point of land between the Rockies and eastern Canada. The hills cover an area of 620 square kilometres, rising abruptly on the west but sloping gently on the east. The top 100 metres of the Cypress Hills is one of the few places in western North America untouched by the last glacial period. The vegetation here is quite varied including some sub-tropical species and types more common in the Rocky Mountains, and some 14 species of orchids. About 200 species of birds and a wide range of other types of animals and wildlife can be found here.

The second highest point of land between the Rocky Mountains and eastern Canada is Mothers Mountain, near Delia. It is 1.3 metres lower than the highest point in the Cypress Hills.

The oldest land surface in Alberta is found in the northeastern part of the province where outcroppings of precambrian era rocks appear. They were formed 600 to 3,500 million years ago. Since that time Alberta has been alternately both dry land and sea, and the remains of the plant and animal life that existed during these various phases contributed to the formation of today's oil, natural gas and coal deposits.

Outcroppings of volcanic rocks occur 13 kilometres east of the B.C. - Alta. border on the Crowsnest Highway. This is the only evidence of volcanic action in Alberta. The rocks consist mostly of cinder and ash, evidence of violent explosion about 100 million years ago.

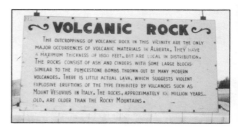

Big Rock, found 10 kilometres west of Okotoks on Highway 7, was deposited there through glacial activity during the last ice age. It is suspected to have come from the Mount Edith Cavell region in Jasper National Park, because of similarities in its composition to rocks of that region. At 18,000 tonnes, it is one of the largest erratics in North America.

The Big Rock

Koroluk Landslide may be reached off Highway 14 east of Wainwright (follow the signs) by going about 19.7 kilometres north and 1.6 kilometres east. This geological phenomenon was formed during heavy rains and run-off in 1974, when an extensive mudslide occurred. Some parts of the field slid down as much as 24 metres.

Koroluk Landslide

Another geological phenomenon in Alberta are known as hoodoos. These odd-looking protrusions are actually the result of erosion occurring over a period of several million years. Three main occurrences are: east of Drumheller; on the Wild Sculpture Trail 65 kilometres northeast of Hinton; and near Banff.

Banff hoodoos

Hinton hoodoos, left

Hoodoos in Drumheller

WATER

Alberta has 16,796 square kilometres of inland water area.

From southeast Alberta the Milk River system drains into the Missouri and Mississippi Rivers which drain into the Gulf of Mexico. Southwest and central Alberta is drained by the South and North Saskatchewan river systems into Hudson's Bay. Northern Alberta is drained by the Athabasca, Hay and Peace rivers into and through the Mackenzie River to the Arctic Ocean.

The largest man-made lake in Alberta is Lake Newell which surrounds Kinbrook Island Provincial Park, near Brooks. It was formed for the Eastern Irrigation District and is the largest block irrigation project in Alberta, irrigating 100,000 hectares of land.

The longest man-made lake in Alberta is Abraham Lake. It was formed by the Big Horn Dam, 91 metres high, a hydro-electric generating project completed in 1972.

Lake Claire and Lesser Slave Lake are the two largest lakes entirely within Alberta and Lesser Slave Lake is the largest auto-accessible lake within the province. It also has the largest sandy beaches in Alberta.

On Highway 1A, west of Lake Louise, is the geographic point where all waters flow either east or west to the Atlantic or Pacific Oceans. Displays describe this phenomenon, called the great divide, at a point where a small creek splits in the middle and half flows in either direction.

At Sunwapta Pass, which forms the boundary between Banff and Jasper national parks, the North Saskatchewan River and the Sunwapta River have their beginnings. Each flows in a different direction: the North Saskatchewan to Hudson's Bay and the Sunwapta to the Arctic.

One of the most outstanding geographical features of the Canadian Rockies is the Columbia Icefield which lies across the Alberta-B.C. border. It covers some 389 square kilometres to depths of up to 910 metres. The Athabasca, Columbia and Saskatchewan Glaciers, forming parts of this icefield, produce meltwaters for

At the great divide

the Mackenzie River (to the Arctic Ocean), the Saskatchewan River (to Hudson's Bay), and the Columbia River (to the Pacific Ocean).
The Columbia Icefield is one of the largest accumulations of snow and ice south of the Arctic Circle, and is the most accessible glacier in North America. It is reached from the Icefields Parkway at Sunwapta Pass, south of Jasper or north of Banff.

Maligne Lake, about an hour's drive from Jasper, is the largest glacial-fed lake in the Canadian Rockies and second largest in the world. It is 23 kilometres long.

The deepest lake in the Rockies is Upper Waterton Lake, in Waterton Lakes National Park, at 142 metres.

Near Fort Chipewyan in northeast Alberta is the Chenal Des Quatre Fourches (Channel of the Four Forks) River. The outstanding and unusual feature of this river is that during high water, in the spring, one of its forks actually reverses its flow.

The eroding power of water is shown in a very picturesque way at Maligne Canyon. The creek at this point has cut through the limestone to a depth of 50 metres at one point, and the canyon it has cut is narrow enough for the squirrels to jump across.

RECORD-SETTING WEATHER

Scientists believe they may have found out why the *aurora borealis* (Northern Lights) appear to undulate in the sky. The lights are formed by sheets of high-energy electrons, travelling outward from the sun, that are pulled into the atmosphere by Earth's magnetic field. The consequent electric fields cause the electrified air on either side to flow rapidly in opposite directions, setting up rippling curtains of light. The colors in the sheet are generated by electrons of different energies hitting molecules of air gases, causing them to glow yellow, green, red and purple. Northern Lights are often seen in Alberta.

Weather forecasts were first published for the prairies on August 26, 1891.

On January 11, 1911 the temperature at Fort Vermilion, Alberta went down to -61.1°C, the lowest temperature ever recorded in Canada outside of the Yukon. (The lowest recorded temperature in the world was at Vostok in the Antarctic on July 21, 1983. It was -89°C.)

On July 30, 1918, three children in Vermilion, Alberta, were killed by a tornado which also destroyed the grandstand at Wainwright's exhibition grounds.

On July 7 & 8, 1927, forty tornados were reported across central Alberta. Over 60 farms lost grain bins, storage sheds, barns and/or homes during this period. Three people were killed and several were injured.

On June 13, 1930, it rained mud at Provost, Alberta. A mixture of blowing dust and heavy rain produced this phenomenon.

July 21, 1931 - The highest temperature ever recorded in Alberta occurred on this date: 43.3°C at Brooks. This same temperature was reached at Fort Macleod on July 18, 1941.

September 24, 1950 - Burning muskeg and forest fires in northern Alberta produced such a massive cloud of smoke that in about two days it was spread over the skies of Europe.

June 5, 1951 - Precipitation combined with freezing temperatures produced a 40 centimetre snow cover over Calgary in 36 hours.

On July 14, 1953, a hailstorm over Alberta killed 36,000 ducks and thousands of other birds, such as owls and songbirds. Four days later, another hailstorm killed 27,000 ducks in the same area.

The greatest snowfall ever to descend on Edmonton was a total of 46 centimetres on April 18 & 19, 1955.

On December 20, 1961 at Lethbridge, Alberta, the temperature went from 3.3°C at 5 a.m. to -19.4°C at 6 a.m. — a drop of 22.7°C in one hour.

The largest ever "summer snowfall" recorded in Canada was on June 29, 1963 at Livingston Ranger Station, Alberta. At that time 111.8 centimetres of snow fell. For many years, this was the greatest one-day snowfall ever recorded in Canada.

On January 7, 1969, one of Edmonton's longest cold snaps began. For 26 consecutive days the temperature remained well below 0°F (-17.8°C), until February 2nd. The coldest day of this period was January 30 at -39.4°C.

The lowest relative humidity ever recorded in Canada was 6 per cent. This was in Calgary, Alberta on March 22, 1968. The temperature at the time was 18 degrees and the dew point was -20 degrees. Calgary's normal relative humidity for this time of year is about 59 per cent.

August 7, 1971 - Baseball-sized hailstones fell for 15 minutes in the area of Whitecourt, Alberta. They were driven by 80 km/h winds at a 45° angle, causing damage to every roof, window and neon sign in the area. Even aluminum roofs and sidings were penetrated, and six planes were destroyed. Twenty-centimetre drifts of hail lay in the area for a couple of days afterwards.

July 6,1975 - A giant hailstone weighing 249 grams fell during a thirteen-minute hailstorm on a farm southwest of Wetaskiwin, Alberta. It was one of the heaviest hailstones documented in Canada to this date.

May 18, 1980 - Mount St. Helens, in Washington State, erupted sending smoke and ash 24 kilometres into the air. The plume reached the east coast in three days and circled the world in 19 days. A thin ash layer fell in the Okanagan Valley and visibility was poor across the prairies.

July 28, 1981 - A severe summer hailstorm lasting only about fifteen minutes over Calgary and the surrounding area did $100 million damage.

May 14-15, 1986 - A two-day blizzard across south central Alberta was accompanied by winds of 80 km/h, and knee-deep snow. It was considered the worst spring storm in the history of the province.

July 19, 1986 - About 900 Edmonton residents were forced to flee their homes as the surging waters of the rain-swollen North Saskatchewan River rose 11.6 metres (7.6 metres above normal), and caused the area's worst flooding since 1915. Two deaths were attributed to the floods. Across northern and central Alberta huge tracts of farmland were flooded. About 80% of the forage crops were submerged.

July 31, 1987 - A series of tornadoes struck eastern Edmonton, killing 27, injuring over 200 and leaving 400 homeless. Termed Canada's largest natural disaster, this "Black Friday" storm blew apart a huge oil tank, threw cars around and toppled transmission towers. Losses were over $250 million, the greatest damage ever done by a single storm in Canada.
Hailstones accompanying the storm reached weights of up to 264 grams, the largest ever recorded in Alberta. (The largest recorded in Canada was 290 grams and the largest ever recorded in North America was 758 grams at Coffeyville, Kansas, on September 3, 1970.)

January 30, 1989 - A snowstorm hit Edmonton and area and set a new one-day record for January. Twenty-nine centimetres of snow broke the old record of 27.9 cm which had been set in 1885.

Hailstones from the Black Friday tornado, courtesy of Henry and Pat Blake of south Edmonton. The coins are loonies.

OTHER WEATHER FACTS

Southern Alberta is well known for its chinook winds. The *Canadian Encyclopedia* gives this information: "Air funnelling through the Rockies produces the warm, dry chinook winds, especially strong and prevalent in southwest Alberta. Chinooks can raise temperatures dramatically in hours."

February 6, 1875 - Dr. Richard Neuitt recorded this description of a chinook at Lethbridge: "Still cold and the snow on the ground is about six inches deep; around 4:30 a strong wind from the west sprang up and in 9 minutes the thermometer had risen 32° from plus 8° to 40°F."

A record temperature change occurred during a chinook on January 27, 1962. The temperature rose from -18°C (0°F) to 3°C (37°F) — a rise of 21°C (37°F) in one hour. There is an average of about ten chinooks each winter in the Crowsnest Pass/Pincher Creek area.

January 6, 1966 - A spectacular temperature change occurred at Pincher Creek, Alberta. Thermometer readings were -24.4°C at 7 a.m., 0.6°C at 8 a.m. and -21.7°C at 9 a.m. The temperature remained steady until 3 p.m. and then rose to 2.2°C for the rest of the day.

Alberta is Canada's sunniest province with averages of 1,900 hours of sunshine annually in the north to 2,300 hours in the south.

According to the 1989 Canadian Weather Trivia Calendar, Manyberries, Alberta, has 2,309 hours of sunshine per year.

The Waterton Lakes area has claimed the distinction of having not only Alberta's warmest winters, but also one of the highest snowfall averages in the province.

The coldest day ever recorded in Edmonton was -49.4°C on January 19, 1886.

Climate Severity Index is a scale from one to 100, which was devised by Environment Canada to rate any particular area's (or locality's) average climate with all conditions being taken into account. Of all the major Canadian cities, Victoria, B.C., was best at 13 and St. John's, Newfoundland, was worst at 56. Calgary came in at 34 and Edmonton at 37 — third and fifth on the list.

According to the Canadian Weather Trivia Calendar, July 11th is outstanding because " . . . more notable weather events occurred on this day than any other." The comments for October 2nd say it is "noteworthy because nothing happened on this day. To the best of our knowledge, this date is devoid of major storms, unseasonal heat or cold waves, or untimely frosts and snows. Today's forecast is for no surprises. Enjoy it!"

March 23rd is World Meteorological Day.

Please note: The above-mentioned Canadian Weather Trivia Calendar was the source of many of the items in this chapter, which are reproduced with permission of the Minister of Supply and Services Canada, 1989.

PARKS

Alberta has 90 species of mammals, 270 species of birds, 50 species of fish, 20 species of reptiles and amphibians, and 1700 types of plants.

The Canadian Parks and Wilderness Society, (formerly known as National and Provincial Parks Association of Canada), is an educational, non-profit organization, incorporated under federal charter in 1963 for the purpose of promoting the protection of national, provincial and territorial wilderness areas and other places of natural significance. It is hoped that through their efforts, Canadians and visitors will develop a personal commitment to preserve, enjoy and benefit from parks, wildlands and natural areas for all time. CPAWS is a member of the International Union for Conservation of Natural Resources. For more information phone (403) 453-8658.

In Canada there are 31 national parks and 70 national historic parks and sites.

PARKS IN ALBERTA

In Alberta there are: five national parks totalling 6,304,676 hectares, sixty-one provincial parks covering 125,418 hectares, four wilderness areas taking up 560,660 hectares and one hundred and one natural areas totalling 31,806 hectares.

The five national parks in this province are:

Banff	Est.1885	6,642 sq. km
Waterton Lakes	Est.1895	526 sq. km
Jasper	Est.1907	10,878 sq. km
Elk Island	Est.1913	194 sq. km
Wood Buffalo	Est.1922	44,807 sq. km

Banff National Park was originally called Rocky Mountain Park when it was established in 1885. It was the first national park in Canada and third in the world. Banff National Park began as a small (26 km²) reservation of land around the mineral hot springs.

The Waterton Lakes were named after Charles Waterton, a mid-nineteenth century naturalist. The original residents of the area, the Kootenai Indians, called the chain of lakes *Onk-se-kimi*, which means "beautiful waters." The Indians called the area of Waterton Lakes "the land of shining mountains."

Waterton Lakes National Park was established in 1895 and in 1932 it joined Glacier National Park in Montana to form the world's first international peace park. In 1979, UNESCO (The United Nations Educational, Scientific and Cultural Organization) recognized the park as a biosphere reserve. The park has about 200 kilometres of hiking trails, some of which connect with trails in the adjoining Glacier National Park.

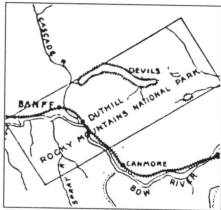
This 1892 map shows the original Banff National Park.

Jasper National Park was established in 1907 and Jasper Park Lodge was built and opened in 1922. Until 1988 the lodge was open only during the summer months. It now remains open year-round. The Jasper Tramway began in 1964 taking people up Whistlers Mountain. To date approximately three million people have enjoyed the lift and the view.

In 1910 Buffalo National Park was established near Wainwright, with a herd of 740 buffalo. In 1913, the herd was moved to Elk Island National Park.

Elk Island National Park was originally established in 1906 as Canada's first federal wildlife sanctuary for large mammals. Elk Island has some of the richest grazing land in North America. More than 229 species of birds and 44 species of mammals inhabit the park's 20,000 hectares.

Wood Buffalo National Park lies across the Alberta - Northwest Territories border and it is home to the largest herd of bison in the world. The park, established December 18, 1922, was formed to accommodate the herd of wood buffalo discovered there by surveyors in 1916. During the years 1925 to 1927, about 6,000 plains buffalo from Wainwright were moved into the park. Wood Buffalo is also home of the nesting grounds for the near-extinct whooping crane.

One of Alberta's greatest scenic attractions, the Columbia Icefield, lies across the boundary of Banff and Jasper National Parks. See the Natural Features section for more on this icefield.

On the west side of Rocky Mountain House is located the only national historic park in Alberta. It commemorates the sites of several original trading posts dating from 1800 and also the history of the Peigan Indians, and David Thompson and the fur trade. (The first national historic park in Canada was established in 1917 in Nova Scotia. These parks commemorate people, places and/or events that played important roles in Canada's development. In 1986, there were 73 major parks and sites and over 900 plaques and monuments at significant sites and about 30 more under development.)

There are 18 cultural and world historic sites in Alberta.

PROVINCIAL PARKS

There are 10 provincial parks in Alberta, covering an area of about 7,700 square kilometres.

Provincial parks are areas of land set aside by provincial governments, within their own jurisdictions, to help conserve the natural environment for the enjoyment of residents and visitors.

William A. Switzer Provincial Park was originally called Entrance Provincial Park. It was renamed after the well known Edson-area MLA of 1965-69.

Kananaskis Provincial Park is the largest provincial park in Alberta (30 km^2) and it is also the first provincial mountain park.

Dinosaur Provincial Park was established in 1955 to protect one of the most extensive dinosaur fields in the world, in both size and number of species of dinosaur remains. Most of the fossils are 70 million years old, from the cretaceous period. This fossil field was discovered in 1889 and since that time almost 120 skeletons and partial skeletons have been uncovered and are in museums around the world. In 1980 the park was proclaimed a world heritage site by the United Nations. The park contains the largest area of badlands in Canada — a unique habitat for some rare and endangered animals and plants. It serves to protect one of the world's richest fossil beds.

The Cypress Hills in southeastern Alberta provide habitat for about 200 species of birds and over 400 plant species including 15 species of orchids. Cypress Hills Provincial Park is the second largest in Alberta and it attracts about 225,000 visitors annually. There have been at least 90 different archaeological sites recognized in the Cypress Hills and some date back 7,000 years. The top 100 metres of the Cypress Hills are one of the few areas of western North America untouched by the glaciers of the last ice age.

James Doty, in 1855, was the first white man to see the sandstone cliffs in southern Alberta which are covered with pictographs and symbols of men, animals, bows, shields, etc. depicting tales of Indian life and lore of long ago. This ancient artwork is now contained within the boundaries of Writing-On-Stone Provincial Park.

Big Knife Provincial Park, northeast of Stettler, is also located in a badlands area.

PROVINCIAL HISTORIC SITES

Dunvegan - Fort Dunvegan was established in 1805 as a major fur and provision post and agricultural site for the Hudson's Bay Company. Company buildings, and the church and rectory, are being restored. It is located on the north side of the Peace River beside Dunvegan Bridge (between Grande Prairie and Peace River).

Fort Dunvegan

Fort McMurray Oil Sands - The Fort McMurray Oil Sands Interpretive Centre has displays depicting the history and development of the oil sands which began in the 1920s.

The entrance of the Fort McMurray Oil Sands Interpretive Centre

Victoria Settlement - Sixteen kilometres south of Smoky Lake, Fort Victoria and the Victoria Methodist Mission have been partially restored. Ongoing restoration projects include the Clerk's Quarters, which was built in 1864 and is now the oldest building in Alberta on its original site.

Clerk's Quarters at Victoria Settlement

Father Lacombe Chapel - This was the first Roman Catholic chapel in St. Albert, and was built by Father Lacombe, with the help of the local Métis, in 1861.

Father Lacombe Chapel, St. Albert

Rutherford House - This Edmonton residence was the home of Alberta's first premier, A.C. Rutherford (1857-1941). Built in 1910-11 at a cost of $25,000, the house was named Achnacarry after the ancestral home of

the Camerons in Scotland. The house was purchased by the government and renovated to its 1915 appearance, to be opened as an historic site in 1973. Guided tours are given by costumed interpreters, including historic dramas, craft and music performances.

Strathcona Archaeological Centre - The remains at this archaeological dig are over 5,000 years old. Visitors can watch archaeologists at work and there is also a volunteer program for anyone interested in digging. Phone (403) 427-5708.

Men of Vision statue at Cochrane Ranch

Ukrainian Cultural Heritage Village - Located about 50 kilometres east of Edmonton on Highway 16, the village is made up of restored homes, shops, churches, etc., from all over Alberta. They are laid out in three displays: an isolated homestead, a rural community and a small town. Together they portray the life of Ukrainian pioneers in Alberta. This project was taken over by the provincial government in 1975 and continues to be expanded today.

Cochrane Ranche - The Cochrane Ranche was the first large-scale ranching operation in Alberta. It was established in 1881 and built up to 144,000 hectares of land containing several thousand head of cattle. The site is now watched over by the famous Men of Vision statue which was put up in commemoration of the working cowboy of early ranching days.

Frank Slide - At the Frank Slide Interpretive Centre, the history of the coal mining industry of the Crowsnest Pass area is featured. With the coming of the railway in 1897 the area boomed. On April 29, 1903, 90 million tons of rock from Turtle Mountain slid and tumbled into the valley below, partially destroying the town of Frank and killing about 70 people.

Rutherford House

Frank Slide and Interpretive Centre

*Head-Smashed -In Buffalo Jump
Interpretive Centre*

Head-Smashed-In Buffalo Jump - This area was designated a world heritage site by UNESCO in 1981. It is a site where, for over 6,000 years, Indians drove herds of bison over the cliff to their deaths, for food, shelter and clothing. This is the largest and best preserved buffalo jump in North America and it received its name in memory of one Indian who got a little too close to the action. It was officially opened by the Duke and Duchess of York on July 23, 1987.

Leitch Collieries - The picturesque ruins of the Leitch Collieries is the setting for the historic site where turn-of-the-century coal mining and processing techniques are explained to visitors.

Leitch Collieries in the Crowsnest Pass

Home of Stephansson - Stephen G. Stephansson was considered one of the greatest poets in Iceland and in the western world. He lived just north of Markerville, where he wrote of his experiences both in Canada and Iceland. The house has been restored to 1920s style.

Stephansson House, Markerville

The Brooks Aqueduct was officially opened on August 5, 1989, as a provincial and national historic site. It is a landmark of civil engineering and agriculture in western Canada.

In the early 1960s, three Alberta wilderness areas were established: Siffleur, White Goat and Ghost River. These areas are protected: they are only accessible on foot, and hunting, fishing and trapping are prohibited.

The Willmore Wilderness Park is 4,600 square kilometres and has 750 kilometres of trails. The park was established in 1959. Motorized access into the area is strictly regulated.

Natural areas are those areas representing one or more aspects of the province's biological and physical diversity, set aside for recreational, educational and/or conservation purposes.

The smallest natural area in Alberta is Antler Lake, which is one hectare in size, and the largest area is The Beehive consisting of 6,700 hectares.

The Kootenay Plains area, along the David Thompson Highway west of the Big Horn Dam, is a former Indian meeting, camping and ceremonial ground. It is also biologically unique, as its climate is moderate although it is a Rocky Mountain pass. This is due to the westerly winds that frequent the area.

Alberta's first provincial historic area was Fort Macleod. Fort Macleod's downtown core is southern Alberta's oldest settlement. Thirty architecturally rich structures dating from the 1890s can be found here, as well as the first North-West Mounted Police post in the west, built in 1874. Today the museum has displays on the early NWMP, the Indians, pioneers, and the times.

Fort Macleod

Pumphouse Theatre, Calgary

Calgary's Pumphouse Theatre was originally built in 1913 as a pumphouse to supply water to the people of Calgary. It was retired from service in 1967. In 1972 it was re-opened as a theatre. This simple brick building was declared an Alberta Historic Site in 1975 and in 1980 was proclaimed Canada's third major national water landmark.

The Atlas Coal Mine at East Coulee, near Drumheller, is the last of its type in Canada. It was established in 1917 and was one of 138 registered mines in the area. The Atlas Coal Mine and Museum are being designated an historic site where you will be able to see first-hand a real coal mine complete with equipment, tipple, washhouse, blacksmith shop, office, beltline and various artifacts.

Fort Normandeau is the reconstructed site of the original settlement of Red Deer. By a natural river crossing long used by Indians and animals, the first settlers opened a store in 1882 and expanded to include a stopping house in 1884. The following year, during the

DAVID THOMPSON.

David Thompson was born in London, England on April 30th 1770. His father died when he was only two years old. He was apprenticed to the Hudsons Bay Company at the age of 14 and sent to Churchill in 1784. He spent 13 years with the Bay serving in posts on Hudsons Bay and in Saskatchewan. He spent the winter of 1787-88 living with Indians in the area of present day Calgary. In May 1797 he left the H.B.C. and joined the rival North West Company. In 1807 he and his family crossed the Rockies by what is now known as Howse Pass. David Thompson was the first white man to travel the full length of the Columbia River. He died in Longueuil near Montreal on Feb. 10th 1857.

Riel Rebellion, it was fortified, for protection, and named Fort Normandeau.

The Frog Lake Massacre Historic Site is located three kilometres east of the Frog Lake Store and was considered a central point on the first trade route trail from Fort Carlton through Fort Pitt toward Edmonton. The first recorded

Fort Normandeau

use of this trail was in 1805. An Indian uprising here in 1885 resulted in the deaths of nine people.

In southwest Lethbridge is Indian Battle Park, at the site of one of the last great Indian battles which was fought in 1870 between the Blackfoot and the Cree.

Stone Pile, a legally protected historic site three kilometres southwest of Rumsey, is a pile of stones left from an old Indian ceremonial ground.

Frog Lake Massacre Site

Atlas Coal Mine

PARKS - MUNICIPAL & MISCELLANEOUS

The North Saskatchewan River Valley, flowing through Edmonton, contains North America's largest and longest expanse of natural parkland in a city. Capital City Recreation Park consists of 2,291 hectares of land on both sides of the river.

The world's only log opera house was built in 1896 at Canmore, Alberta. Many internationally famous stars and groups played here, including Jack Benny, the British National Opera, and the International Welsh Choir. Canmore Mines donated the building to Calgary's Heritage Park in 1966. It was dismantled, and then transported and rebuilt at the park. Today it is a year-round centre for old-style entertainment.

Log Opera House - Heritage Park, Calgary

Heritage Park, Calgary

Calaway Park on Highway 1

Heritage Park at Calgary is Canada's largest "living history" village. Featured is an authentic fur-trading fort, a turn-of-the-century town, a farming community, steam trains, street cars, vintage vehicles, antique midway rides and costumed staff.

Gateway Park - The Imperial Leduc No. 1 Oil Derrick was erected here as a monument to the pioneers in oil exploration, and commemorating the oil strike near Leduc on February 13, 1947. Located at 51st Avenue from 1958 to 1983, the derrick was moved to its present site at Gateway Park in 1987. An oil interpretive display is located in the adjacent visitor information centre.

The largest sundial in Canada is located in the Bud Miller All Seasons Park in Lloydminster. It is the second largest sundial in North America, measuring 60 metres across.

Calgary has over 250 kilometres of well groomed trails for cyclists and hikers alike.

The largest sundial in Canada is located in Lloydminster.

Gateway Park Visitor Centre, Edmonton

THE METRIC SYSTEM

In Canada, all measurements are made using the metric system. Rain, snowfall, windspeed and visibility are expressed in metric units. Temperature is calculated on the Celsius scale. All distance markers and road speed signs are in kilometres (km) and kilometres per hour (km/h). Gasoline and other liquid volumes or commodities are measured in litres.

For normal, average, everyday use, there are three basic units of measurement in the metric system: the metre, the gram and the litre.

The metre (m) is used for measuring lengths and distances.
The gram (g) is used for measuring weights and mass.
The litre is used for measuring capacity.

A 10-centimetre cube will hold 1 litre of water and it will weigh 1 kilogram. There are six numerical prefixes which can be used in conjunction with the three basic units named above. These are:

milli, meaning one-thousandth (1/1000 or 0.001)
centi, meaning one-hundredth (1/100 or 0.01)
deci, meaning one-tenth (1/10 or 0.1)
deka, meaning ten (10)
hecto, meaning one hundred (100)
kilo, meaning one thousand (1000)

And again for normal, average, everyday use, only three prefixes will likely be needed: milli, centi and kilo. For measuring lengths and distances all three are in common use: millimetre (mm), centimetre (cm) and kilometre (km). The metre consists of 1000 mm or 100 cm — it's just a matter of moving the decimal point.

The push buttons on a telephone are 1 cm square (1 cm²).
The *TV Guide* measures approximately 13 cm by 19 cm.
The standard egg carton is about 30 cm long.

ANNIVERSARIES

	Traditional	Modern
First	Paper	Clocks
Second	Cotton	China
Third	Leather	Crystal, Glass
Fourth	Fruit, Flowers	Appliances
Fifth	Wood	Silverware
Sixth	Candy, Iron	Wood
Seventh	Wool, Copper	Desk Sets
Eighth	Bronze, Pottery	Linens, Laces
Ninth	Pottery, Willow	Leather
Tenth	Tin, Aluminum	Diamond Jewelry
Eleventh	Steel	Fashion Jewelry
Twelfth	Silk, Linen	Pearls
Thirteenth	Lace	Textiles, Furs
Fourteenth	Ivory	Gold Jewelry
Fifteenth	Crystal	Watches
Twentieth	China	Platinum
Twenty-fifth	Silver	Silver
Thirtieth	Pearl	Diamond
Thirty-fifth	Coral	Jade
Fortieth	Ruby	Ruby
Forty-fifth	Sapphire	Sapphire
Fiftieth	Gold	Gold
Fifty-fifth	Emerald	Emerald
Sixtieth	Diamond	Diamond
Seventy-fifth	Diamond	Diamond

The front page of the Edmonton Sun newspaper measures approximately 29 cm by 38 cm.

The front page of the Edmonton Journal measures approximately 35 cm by 60 cm.

The 26-inch TV screen is about 52 cm by 40 cm.

The average doorway is about 2 metres high.

For longer distances the kilometre is used. This is one thousand metres and is equal to 8 to 10 average city blocks.

For measuring weight we normally only use the basic unit of grams (g), and kilograms (kg).

An average loaf of bread is about 450 g.

The *TV Guide* weighs about 100 g.

A desk telephone is about 2 kg (or 2000 g).

An average man is 165 to 180 cm in height and weighs 70 to 80 kg.

You may use milligrams (mg) when dealing with medicines. An average aspirin tablet weighs about 325 mg or approximately one-third of a gram.

For measuring capacities we will use mainly the litre (L) and/or millilitre (ml).

A teaspoon holds 5 ml.

A cup contains 250 ml (1/4 of a litre).

An average can of pop contains 355 ml.

A bottle of beer contains 341 ml.

The gas tank of the average car holds 50 to 60 L.

A barrel contains 205 L.

There is one more unit of measurement that concerns us in everyday use: temperature. This is measured in degrees celsius (°C). In this system, 0°C is the freezing point of water and 100°C is the boiling point.

A nice spring day would be 15° - 20°C.
A hot day would be 30°C and over.
Normal body temperature is 37°C.
A slow oven would be around 130°C.
A very hot oven would be around 275°C.

BIRTHSTONES AND FLOWERS

January	Garnet	Carnation
February	Amethyst	Violet
March	Aquamarine	Jonquil
April	Diamond	Sweet Pea
May	Emerald	Lily of the Valley
June	Pearl	Rose
July	Ruby	Larkspur
August	Peridot	Gladiolus
September	Sapphire	Aster
October	Opal	Calendula
November	Topaz	Chrysanthemum
December	Turquoise	Narcissus

STATUTORY HOLIDAYS IN ALBERTA

New Year's Day	January 1
Family Day	third Monday of February
Good Friday	Friday preceding Easter
Victoria Day	Monday preceding May 24
Canada Day	July 1
Heritage Day	first Monday in August
Labour Day	first Monday in September
Thanksgiving	second Monday in October
Remembrance Day	November 11
Christmas Day	December 25
Boxing Day	December 26

There is one point on the scales where the Fahrenheit and Celsius temperatures are the same: at minus 40 degrees.

As you no doubt noticed I purposely left out the scales for converting from one system to the other. The reason for this is simple: the best way to learn metric is to think metric. Use the above examples, or make up some of your own, for comparision purposes, and you should soon discover that it is not all that hard or complicated.

MESSAGES AND CONGRATULATIONS

If you or someone you know is celebrating one of the following events, messages and congratulations can be received from:

Her Majesty the Queen, for anniversaries of 60 years or more and birthdays of 100 years or more.

The Governor General, for anniversaries from 50 to 59 years and birthdays from 90 to 99 years.

The Prime Minister, for anniversaries of 50 years or more and birthdays of 70 years or more.

The Lieutenant Governor, for anniversaries of 50 years or more and birthdays of 70 years or more.

The Premier of the province, for anniversaries of 50 years or more and birthdays of 70 years or more.

Requests for these must be made well in advance. For more information contact your local MP or MLA or write (postage free) to the House of Commons, Ottawa, Ontario, or to the Provincial Secretary's Office, c/o the Legislature Building in Edmonton.

QUIZ ANSWERS

1. Beaverlodge 2. Hairy Hill 3. Cereal 4. Nojack 5. Carstairs 6. Castor 7. Woking 8. Alliance 9. Blackfoot 10. Dunmore 11. Entrance 12. Duchess 13. Red Deer 14. Bragg Creek 15. Veteran 16. Foremost 17. High Level 18. Freedom 19. North Star 20. Grand Centre 21. College Heights 22. Big Valley 23. Legal 24. Bonanza 25. Coronation 26. Bluesky 27. Stand Off 28. Calling Lake 29. Fairview 30. Milk River 31. Medicine Hat 32. Reno 33. Consort 34. Viking 35. Champion 36. Redcliff 37. Canmore 38. Gift Lake 39. Longview 40. Michichi

41. Sir James Alexander Lougheed (grandfather of former Alberta premier, Edgar Peter Lougheed).
42. Moraine Lake (near Lake Louise) in the Canadian Rockies.
43. Mt. Columbia, at 3,747 metres
44. The Slave River at the Northwest Territories border
45. These are the two main glaciers of the Columbia Icefield.
46. St. Albert and Edmonton
47. Sir James Lougheed (see also number 41)
48. Young Woman's Christian Association (YWCA)
49. Health, Hope, Happiness
50. If anyone knows this one please let me know (see page 90 for correspondence address).

UPDATES, REVISIONS
AND ADDITIONS

Do you want to challenge items of trivia included in this book? Do you have items which could be included in future editions?
In either case please let me know.
For revisions, please note: the chapter number, the page number, how the item reads, how it should read and where this point can be verified.
For additions, please note: where the point can be verified.

All correspondence should be sent to:

DON BLAKE
9602 - 162 Street
Edmonton, Alberta
T5P 3K8

A laminated trivia map, approximately 22 x 37 inches, is also available from Don Blake for $2.95 retail.

BIBLIOGRAPHY

The following sources were referred to in compiling the information contained in this book:

PUBLICATIONS
A Brief History of Dres (CFB Suffield)
Alberta Breaks
Alberta Culture (brochure)
Alberta Discovery Guide
Alberta Facts
Alberta Film and Literary Arts Bulletin
Alberta Gets Tough on Impaired Drivers (pamphlet from the Solicitor General's Department of the Alberta Government)
Alberta Government Road Map
Alberta Municipalities (pamphlet)
Alberta Native News
Alberta On Ice (book)
Alberta Past (newspaper)
Alberta Provincial Parks (brochures, pamphlets)
Alberta Report
Alberta Sports Council
Alberta Touring Guide
Alberta's Local Governments (book by Walter Walchuk for Alberta Municipal Affairs, 1987)

Banff-Lake Louise Lift (brochure by North Hill News, Calgary)
Brooks (brochure)
Building the Promise (sports brochure)

Calaway Park (brochures)
Camp Wainwright (booklet)
Can You Dig It?
Canada Handbook
Canadian Encyclopedia
CFL '88 (book)
Canadian Parks and Wilderness Society (forestry newsletter)

Canadian Weather Trivia Calendar (from Minister of Supply and Services, Canada)
Canadian World Almanac (book)
Cardston, Town of (brochures)
Commerce News, The

Drillsite News (magazine)
Drumheller (brochure)

Edmonton Art Gallery (brochures)
Edmonton Examiner, The
Edmonton Journal, The
Edmonton Space Sciences Centre (brochures)
Edmonton Sun, The
Edmonton Talks (brochure)
Edmonton . . . The Way It Was (book)
Edmonton - Trading Post to Metropolis (book by City of Edmonton Anniversaries Committee of Public Relations Bureau)
Experience the Past (brochure)
Expo '86 Trivia

Forestry Forum (Autumn/Winter 1987-88 Canadian Forestry Service)
Fort McMurray Visitor's Guide
Funk and Wagnall's Dictionary

Gateway to Adventure (visitor's guide)
Great Alberta Breaks (by Alberta Tourism)
Grow With Us (brochure)

Henderson's Alberta Directory
Heritage Day News
Hinton (brochure)

Jasper Booster, The

Kangaroo Rats and Rattlesnakes (booklet published by CFB Suffield)

Klondike Days Official Guide

Legislative Tours (brochure)
Lethbridge, City of (brochure)
Luck Magazine (Western Canada Lottery Corporation)

Medicine Hat (brochure)

National and Historic Parks Guide
NHL Official Guide and Record Book
National Parks (brochures, pamphlets)
Neighbor's News (Edmonton)
New Westminster Columbian Newspaper

Oil Sands (brochure)
Oldman River Dam (brochure)
Olympic Saddledome, Calgary (brochure)

Place Names of Alberta (by Eric and Patricia Holmgren, 1976: Western Producer Prairie Books, Saskatoon, Saskatchewan)
Provincial Historic Sites (brochures, pamphlets)
Provincial Museum of Alberta (various brochures)
Private Advertising

Red Barn (brochure by Alberta Wildlife Park)
Red Deer Guide (brochure)
Royal Bank Reporter (news bulletin of the Royal Bank of Canada)

Short Grass Country, CFB Suffield (booklet)
Sight Seeing Tours of Edmonton (brochures)
StatsCan (booklet)
Stony Plain (brochure)

Storyteller (provincial museum news)
Strathcona County (book)
Strathcona Plaindealer (newsletter of
Old Strathcona Foundation)
Sylvan Summer News

The Best of Calgary
The Cornerstone (AHRF News)
The Telephone (AGT booklet)
This Is Beautiful British Columbia
(book by Don Blake)
Tourism Pulse
Tourist Brochures (various)
Tourist Zone Brochures
Travel Alberta Accommodations Guide
Travel Guide (Edmonton Sun, written
by Guy Demarino)

Truckside Advertising
Turtle Times News (Frank Slide)

U.N. Human Rights (brochure)

Vancouver Province, The
Vancouver Sun, The
Visions '89 (The Edmonton Sun)
Visitors Guide to the Legislature

Western Regional Newspapers
(supplement)
Wish You Were Here (advertising)
World Almanac (book)
Wrigley's Alberta Directory
Writing Local History (booklet by
Alberta Culture)

Yellowhead Highway Road Map

OTHER SOURCES
Alberta Experience (TV Show)
Forestry Coming of Age (TV Show)
road signs
television newscasts (various)
private advertising
local information booths

Also see the list of people and places
that provided information for the book,
under the acknowledgements section.

ABOUT THE AUTHOR

Don Blake was born and raised in British Columbia. He worked in construction, in the trucking industry, and as a longshoreman and a prospector, before becoming a writer. He also served with the RCAF. His previous books are: *Blakeburn: From Dust to Dust*, a history of a coal mining town; *This is Beautiful British Columbia*, a best-selling book of B.C. trivia; and *The Valley of the Ghosts*, a history of a section of the West Kootenays. He has just taken on the position of Book Display Coordinator with the Writers Guild of Alberta.

The author, after searching for some weather trivia (also shoveling snow off walk) in -30 degrees celcius temperature.